THE GUTSY GIRL Handbook

ALSO BY KATE WHITE

NONFICTION

I Shouldn't Be Telling You This: How to Ask for the Money,
Snag the Promotion, and Create the Career You Deserve

Why Good Girls Don't Get Ahead but Gutsy Girls Do

FICTION

Even If It Kills Her

The Secrets You Keep

The Wrong Man

Eyes on You

So Pretty It Hurts

The Sixes

Hush

Lethally Blond

Over Her Dead Body

'Til Death Do Us Part

A Body to Die For

If Looks Could Kill

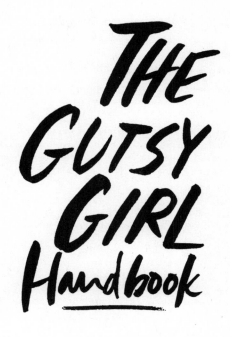

THE GUTSY GIRL Handbook

Your Manifesto for Success

KATE WHITE

GRAND CENTRAL
Life & Style
NEW YORK · BOSTON

To Diane Kordas, fabulous jewelry designer, fantastic friend,
and one of my favorite gutsy girls on the planet.

———

Grand Central Life & Style
Hachette Book Group
1290 Avenue of the Americas
New York, NY 10104
grandcentrallifeandstyle.com
twitter.com/grandcentralpub

First Edition: April 2018

Grand Central Life & Style is an imprint of Grand Central Publishing.
The Grand Central Life & Style name and logo are trademarks of Hachette Book Group, Inc.

The publisher is not responsible for websites (or their content) that are not owned by the publisher.

The Hachette Speakers Bureau provides a wide range of authors for speaking events. To find out more, go to www.hachettespeakersbureau.com or call (866) 376-6591.

Library of Congress Cataloging-in-Publication Data
Names: White, Kate, 1949 August 3–author.
Title: The gutsy girl handbook : your manifesto for success / Kate White.
Description: First Edition. | New York : Grand Central Life & Style, 2018.
Identifiers: LCCN 2017041736| ISBN 9781538711576 (hardback) |
    ISBN 9781478992127 (audio download) | ISBN 9781538711569 (ebook)
Subjects: LCSH: Self-actualization (Psychology) | Motivation (Psychology) |
    Success. | BISAC: SELF-HELP / Personal Growth / Success. | BUSINESS &
    ECONOMICS / Workplace Culture. | SELF-HELP / Motivational &
    Inspirational. | SOCIAL SCIENCE / Women's Studies.
Classification: LCC BF637.S4 W455 2018 | DDC 158—dc23
LC record available at https://lccn.loc.gov/2017041736

ISBNs: 978-1-5387-1157-6 (hardcover), 978-1-5387-1156-9 (ebook)

Printed in the United States of America

LSC-H

10 9 8 7 6 5 4 3 2 1

Contents

I'm going to start off this book with a question for you. It's a pretty simple question, involving only an A or B answer, and yet your response can clue you in to something important about yourself. And, actually, it can do more than that. Understanding the reasons behind your answer could end up changing your whole career trajectory, making it possible for you earn a fatter salary, move ahead more quickly, attain the kind of leadership role in your company and field that you've dreamed about, and feel truly satisfied in your professional life.

Sound good? Okay, so here goes:

When you were offered your current position (even if it's your *first* job) and were informed of the salary you'd be earning, how (roughly) did you respond? A or B?

A. "Thank you so much. I'd really love to join your company. When would you like me to start?"
B. "Thank you so much. I'd really love to join your company. But based on my level of skill and experience and what I can bring to the position, I was looking for X amount."

If you answered B, congratulations. You took a gutsy approach to the discussion, treating it as a negotiation. And I bet it paid off for you. That's because in many cases, a company will initially offer you a lowball salary number, trying to cut the best deal possible as well as allow room for negotiation, which is often expected. Maybe you didn't receive the full amount you wanted, but there's a good chance you gained *something*. Studies show that those who ask for more money when they're being offered a job tend to increase their salaries.

And after asking for more, you hopefully went a step further, determining what perks could be attached to the position—like a signing bonus (more common than many people realize), tuition reimbursement for future studies, a company car, or extra time off. Employers often don't hand those out until you *ask* for them. (Ideally, you also made absolutely certain you were receiving the title, responsibilities, and resources you had anticipated.)

If you answered A, however, you *didn't* negotiate. Instead of being gutsy, you handled the salary discussion like a good girl. You accepted the first amount offered, which means you landed the job but missed the opportunity to end up with a higher salary and/or with valuable perks and/or even enhanced responsibilities.

Understanding the Good Girl Instinct

"Hold on," you may be thinking. "There was a totally legit reason I didn't press for more." Such as:

- I didn't want to seem difficult or greedy and start off on the wrong foot.
- They'd mentioned their budget was tight and I wanted to be respectful of that.

- I'm still early in my career and I figured a few dollars more wasn't worth rocking the boat for.
- The offer was really good. Better than I'd expected.

All of those reasons sound valid and yet they're generally just excuses. They're your good girl instinct overriding the part of your brain that wants a better package and knows you deserve it. You may have been influenced by good girl messaging you heard over time from parents, teachers, and/or society in general. The idea of asking for more made you uncomfortable or concerned about the ramifications, so on some level you tried to justify your decision to accept the amount on the table.

I'm not trying to beat up on you. Plenty of women will answer A. But it's important to be aware of when your good girl instincts kick in and what they can cost you. And it's not just money. Being a good girl can prevent you from achieving the success that you not only yearn for *but are entitled to.*

Take the Good Girl Quiz

Perhaps you're thinking that failing to negotiate was just a momentary loss of nerve and that in general you take a pretty gutsy approach to stuff. See how you respond to these questions.

Yes/No

☐ ☐ Was your last raise what you'd hoped for?

☐ ☐ Are you known, respected, and even envied for having a strong and unique set of professional skills?

☐ ☐ Has your boss responded "Wow" to one of your ideas in the last three weeks?

☐ ☐ Do you get the top assignments?

☐ ☐ Do you know how to pitch ideas in meetings so they're both acknowledged and green-lighted?

☐ ☐ Can you give a killer presentation?

☐ ☐ Are you adept at effectively confronting someone who tries to poach one of your ideas or projects?

☐ ☐ Would your boss consider you a change agent?

☐ ☐ Have you taken a risk lately that paid off big?

☐ ☐ Do you do a good job of not obsessing about issues (and people) at work, and when you do have cause to worry, are you able to keep any anxiety from showing?

☐ ☐ Have you been tapped to be included in special leadership training or mentorship programs in your company?

☐ ☐ Has your boss indicated that you're on the fast track in the department and a good candidate for promotion?

☐ ☐ Do you find your work stimulating and rewarding?

If you answered no to even a couple of these questions, your good girl instincts may be responsible. And those same instincts may be holding you back in bigger ways than you imagined.

Don't worry, you've come to the right place. This book will show you how to burn off those good girl instincts and take a far gutsier approach going forward—in all of the important areas of your career.

Even if you have a track record of making bold moves, this book has lots to offer you. Despite how much the world has changed for women, society still sets up plenty of barriers to success, and it's critical to repeatedly remind yourself how essential it is to let your gutsy side rule.

What's So Damn Bad about Being Good?

Is there really such a downside to being a good girl? Don't nice girls actually finish first in the end? Well, if there is anything I've learned building my personal brand, working in media for decades, and running a top women's magazine for fourteen years, it's that good girls don't get ahead.

They don't get the big promotions. They don't get the corner office. And they don't make six-figure salaries. (At least in most cases they don't.)

Why not?

Because good girls hold back, convinced they're not ready. They undersell themselves in all sorts of situations. They worry about not being liked. They don't ask for what they want. And they're afraid to take risks and break the rules.

The big prizes go to *gutsy* women. Women who don't worry about being perfect or 100 percent ready or liked by everyone. Who own their ambition and excellence. Who ask for what they want. Who take risks and dare to break the rules.

Don't get me wrong. I'm not saying that being gutsy instead of good is the same as being bad. I'm not encouraging you to cheat on your T&E, undermine a colleague, or lie to get ahead. I'm also not suggesting you be brash, rude, or reckless. Rather, this book is about simply taking a bolder, grittier, gutsier approach in your quest for career success.

Twenty-three years ago, I wrote a book called *Why Good Girls Don't Get Ahead but Gutsy Girls Do*. In it I laid out nine strategies that I believed could help women override their good girl tendencies and go after what they wanted in a big way. Those strategies were based not only on what I'd gleaned during my media career, but also on the experiences of many successful women from different fields whom I'd either met along the way or interviewed for the book. There was even a section called, yup... "Lean In."

Part of what inspired me to write the book was realizing how much becoming gutsier had helped my own career. I'd always had gutsy instincts. In fact, my senior year in college, I'd won *Glamour* magazine's "Top Ten College Women" contest in part by ignoring the contest rules. Anyone entering was told to write an essay about her goals for the future, and in an attempt to stand out from the pack, I wrote provocatively about why I had *no* goals (well, I did, of course, and I eventually spelled that out after the catchy beginning). It was one of my first realizations that going against the grain could pay off. But early in my career, I began to tamp down some of those instincts, worried how people in the work world would respond. It took time for me to see that being good only gets you so far and that acting gutsy *always* pays off in the end. I wanted to share what I'd learned with other women.

The book, I'm happy to say, became a bestseller and a bible for many working women. Hundreds of them wrote to me about how much the book had changed their professional lives—or on occasion they even approached me in person. One of the best moments for me was when I was shopping in a Williams-Sonoma one afternoon and a woman in her thirties whom I'd never met walked up to me and said, "Thanks for the $40,000 raise." Boy, did *that* make my week.

As much as I loved the response, I honestly thought the book would have a short shelf life. In fact, the last paragraph read: *And though I know my publisher won't like this, I hope this book is totally obsolete by the time my daughter launches her career.* And it seemed I had good reason to believe that. The world was changing, women were changing, and I was pretty sure that in two decades, there'd be no need for a book on how to be gutsier.

Well, my daughter is now twenty-eight, and though women have made incredible advances, we still face plenty of hurdles. Consider these discouraging stats:

- A recent analysis by Earnest of more than 18,000 jobs across a variety of industries found that "women earn a median of 92 cents on the dollar compared to men. But when women enter *management*, or any role that involves a supervisory capacity over people or teams, they earn just 83 cents for every dollar earned by their male peers."
- According to data compiled by the nonprofit Catalyst, while women accounted for 44 percent of all employees at S&P 500 companies, just 25 percent of executive or senior-level official or managerial positions were held by women. Females held only 9.5 percent of top earning jobs, and only 4.2 percent of CEO positions.
- And though Beyoncé may sing about how girls "run the world," as of this writing, her line of fragrances is made and marketed by a company with only one woman on its executive team and one woman on its board—and they were added recently.

But it's more than just stats that are a concern. When I speak around the country at companies and conferences, I have the chance to chat afterward with women in a wide variety of fields at many different levels of achievement. Many tell me they love what they're doing and are incredibly validated by their careers, but at the same time they may feel frustrated or even stymied.

It may be because of the culture they work in. They encounter roadblocks and bias (sometimes unconscious, sometimes not), particularly if the field is still male dominated. Did you watch the videos of Senator Kamala Harris of California being rudely interrupted and chastised by a couple of male colleagues during two 2017 Senate hearings? I don't think there's a woman in the world who hasn't at some point been interrupted, talked over, shushed, or chided by a male colleague.

Sometimes the women I meet are frustrated because they're still not exactly sure how to play the game. They wonder how aggressively they should go after jobs or promotions (so that there's no risk of their actions backfiring), how to present themselves assertively to peers and subordinates without being seen as a bitch, and what tactics they need to use to break out of middle management. I recently spoke at a large corporation (one that's a household name) where women told me how management is constantly going on and on about all the opportunities there are for employees, but it never happens for any of *them*!

The women I speak with are eager for strategies that will help them get noticed, navigate office politics, come across effectively, earn a bigger paycheck, be seriously considered for the C-suite, and handle those moments when their hard-won confidence inexplicably gets up and leaves the building.

I've come to realize that women can still benefit from the strategies I presented in my book twenty-three years ago. In light of this, the publisher and I decided it was time to revise *Why Good Girls Don't Get Ahead but Gutsy Girls Do* for both a new generation of women and for former readers who would love a refresher course. It's now in a short handbook format, the perfect size for tucking into your bag or desk drawer.

These strategies are appropriate regardless of your age or professional level. They make sense even if you're a millennial who has entered the workplace with a healthy supply of confidence. "Millennials expect to do what they set out to do, and that's a good thing," says Jane Buckingham, CEO of the research and trend-spotting company Trendera and an expert on Gen X, Gen Y, and Gen Z. "Having a sense of entitlement makes you forward thinking and demanding and less likely to settle the way women might have done in the past. But underneath that energy and enthusiasm, there may be a lack of experience and skill, which can cause you to doubt yourself in key moments. You wonder, 'How am I going to go up and *do* that?' I often see millennials hesitate or clutch, particularly in the final ten seconds of a challenging situation."

A friend of mine who recruits candidates in the worlds of finance and IT raises another point. "I see a wonderful level of gutsiness in young women today, but it isn't always strategic. If you're twenty-nine and suddenly managing a fifty-six-year-old guy, you can't just be blindly gutsy. You have to handle things in a way that will get you the best results."

This book will show you how to harness your gutsiness so that it's always working *for* you.

Being gutsier isn't going to fix all the problems you face in your career. It won't stop men from trying to interrupt you in meetings or companies from trying to pay you less than your male counterparts, but it will provide you with strategies for confronting those situations. It will show you how to snag bigger raises, promotions, and opportunities; handle yourself well when the going gets tough; and thrive in your career. When you do something you love and are rewarded for it, it's a very satisfying and often thrilling experience.

Here's something funny I've never mentioned to anyone before. Writing the original *Gutsy Girl* book actually made *me* gutsier. The research clarified certain points for me and provided opportunities to hear terrific strategies from other women that I could borrow when necessary. Sometimes when I needed a kick in the ass, I even went back and reread the book and made sure I was really adhering to the principles I espoused.

Shortly after the book was published, I landed the job as editor in chief of *Redbook* at the Hearst Corporation, and four years later management tapped me to become the editor in chief of *Cosmopolitan*. It was an incredibly exciting job but also very demanding, and to succeed, I relied on every one of the gutsy strategies I'd written about. During my tenure, I increased circulation by 30 percent and took *Cosmo* to number one on the newsstand, keeping it there until I resigned. I also oversaw the *Cosmo* website, *Cosmo* Books, and many other brand extensions.

As much as I loved my job, I made a decision to leave six years ago. I've always been a bit of an outdoor cat and I wanted, while I still had the chance, to try a more entrepreneurial life. That was a gutsy move, too, but I couldn't be happier. I write murder mysteries and thrillers and I speak on leadership and success around the country. Most of the year I live in New York City, but my husband and I spend each winter at our house in Uruguay. That's what I consider freedom at its best.

The nine gutsy girl principles paid off brilliantly for me and I know they will work for you as well. (Just FYI, I've modified and updated all of them.) Over time I think you'll see that they're more than just strategies. They're a manifesto for success that will transform your professional life and can even be used nicely in your personal life as well. Deciding to be gutsy and following through will make you stronger and more confident, and reinforce your instinct to be even gutsier going forward. You'll find it easier to be all that you can be and even reinvent yourself one day if you so desire, or stage the best possible comeback if you temporarily lose your way.

The rumble starts today. Right here, right now. Time to be gutsy as hell.

CHAPTER 1

A Gutsy Girl Breaks the Rules

I always pay attention when I hear successful people talking about their careers, just in case there's a tip I can steal and use for myself. Not long after I landed my first editor in chief job, I was at an event where I overheard Helen Gurley Brown, the legendary editor in chief of *Cosmopolitan* (I had no idea then that I would one day follow in her footsteps!) discussing success, and my ears perked up. I probably even started taking notes.

"The difference between successful people and unsuccessful ones," she said as I waited eagerly for the answer, "is that successful people just work harder."

The members in the group she was talking to nodded in agreement. But you know what? I didn't buy what she said at all—and it still doesn't ring true for me.

Don't get me wrong. I think hard work is always part of the success equation. Very few people end up in fabulous and/or powerful positions without plenty of passion, grit, and perseverance. But to really make your mark, I think it takes more than that. When I look at my own achievements—and those of very successful people I know—it always comes down to **going big or going home**. It's not enough to do what you've been told to do, do it well, and work your butt off in the process. You've got to generate bold, innovative, possibly disruptive ideas and solutions for your company, ideas that break the so-called rules, grow business, increase profitability, set you apart from the pack, and make your boss say "Wow."

And when you're running a department or an entire company, you need a vision that involves plenty of go-big ideas.

Look at Helen! She didn't simply work harder than everyone around her. In 1965 she took a general interest magazine called *Cosmopolitan*, which was limping along on its last legs, and turned it into *Cosmo*, a bold, daring, candid, and stunningly successful publication for women, unlike anything they'd ever seen before. She even featured the first male centerfold—Burt Reynolds on a bearskin rug. That guy was so hairy, you couldn't tell where he ended and the rug began, but women loved it and the magazine blew off newsstands every month. Helen was the master of going big or going home.

When was the last time you made your boss say, "Wow"? When was the last time you came up with a bold new idea or strategy, perhaps something really out of the box, that ran against the way things had always been done in your department or field? It doesn't have to be on par with inventing Facebook (though wouldn't *that* be nice!). Just something that caught everyone's attention because it was fresh and inventive and ended up reaping financial rewards for your company.

If you can't think of anything, it's time to get busy and start going big. Doing what you're told and doing it well will get you so far, maybe even into middle management, but it won't earn you a big position or salary.

I know, I know. Going big isn't easy, is it? If you're a good girl, it runs against your instinct to stay inside the lines and not break any rules. And that's why we often resist doing it.

Good girl instincts, however, aren't the only impediment to big ideas. Busyness is, too. When we're crazed with work and our days are in danger of getting away from us, there's a tendency to revert to the mean and tackle things the same old way they've always been done.

How do you keep these factors from tamping you down? Over time I've found that the best way to guarantee you always go big is to be very systematic about it. It's true that creativity often occurs serendipitously, but I believe you can also generate ideas and insights methodically. I rely on a process I created that makes me examine everything I'm working on and determine how to take it to a bolder level. I'm pretty sure it will be an asset for you, too.

The Special Process for Generating Fabulously Big Ideas

I call my process **the four B's**. You can use it on projects, ideas, and events. It's a ridiculously simple strategy, but it always gets results.

Okay, so here's how it works. You step back from what you're working on, you ask yourself these four critical questions, and then you answer them using specific examples.

1. **Could it be better?**
2. **Could it be bigger?**
3. **Could it be bolder?**
4. **Could it be more *badass*?**

Yes, **badass**, because so often the breakthrough ideas go against the rules and the way things have always been done.

I'll give you an example from my days at *Cosmo* so you can

see how beautifully this process works. When I was headed to work one morning, I heard on the radio that the fastest growing cancer for women in their twenties was melanoma. Gee, I'd had no idea. And do you know why the rate had exploded? In part because of tanning bed use. I decided to warn readers about the problem in the very next issue.

But later I started asking myself: Could I go even *bigger* with this? I decided to run not just one item but an item in *every single* issue and make it part of a campaign we called "Practice Safe Sun." We even introduced the Annual Practice Safe Sun Awards, which were presented each year at a big luncheon.

I didn't stop there, though. I kept asking myself if I could go even bigger and bolder. We approached the ABC news show *20/20* and inquired if they'd be open to doing an investigative report on tanning salons with us. They loved the idea and went ahead with it. Then I called my congresswoman, told her about the issue, and asked if she'd consider introducing legislation that might help. She introduced the Tan Act, which would require a more prominent warning on tanning beds.

Five years later, here were some of the results of the Practice Safe Sun (PSS) Campaign: In a major survey, more than 50 percent of our readers told us they'd changed their sunbathing habits because of PSS. The Tan Act passed and led to other legislation. And the awesome *Cosmo* sales team had sold millions of dollars' worth of advertising pages to companies that wanted to be aligned with PSS.

Going big had paid off big.

Going big can pay off big for you, too. Use the following diagram to help you blow out any idea you're currently developing or project you're spearheading.

The Four B's

1. Ask Yourself
↓

2. Go-Big Answers
↓

Could it be better?

How? What would
really improve it?

———————————
———————————
———————————

Could it be bigger?

What are the possible
add-ons? How could you
give it legs?

———————————
———————————
———————————

Could it be bolder?

How could you color
outside the lines?

———————————
———————————
———————————

Could it be more badass?

What would happen if you turned
the idea on its head and did it a totally
different way?

———————————
———————————
———————————

Two Go-Big Caveats

1. First and foremost, going big must advance your boss's and organization's agendas, not simply your own (but ideally you can kill two birds with one stone).
2. You can't always wait for someone to give you permission. You just have to do it. Like the saying goes, it's better to ask for forgiveness than permission. I love how, following the 2017 Charlottesville riots, Baltimore mayor Catherine E. Pugh relied on her emergency powers to have the city's Confederate statues removed during the middle of the night instead of becoming entangled in bureaucratic red tape. "I thought that there's enough grandstanding, enough speeches," she said at a news conference. "Get it done."

Being a rule breaker is often less renegade than it sounds. Many "rules" are in existence because they once worked quite nicely, but there's every chance they have become meaningless over time. People follow them out of habit, because "that's the way we've always done things here." Other rules or guidelines have been set up by well-meaning people who unfortunately lack skill, talent, or creativity. Some of these rules are just begging to be broken.

How to Create a Big Idea out of Thin Air

Sometimes going big isn't a matter of taking an existing idea and making it bolder. You may not *have* an existing idea to work with and you need to come up with something from scratch. Daunting, right?

There's actually a great strategy for coming up with a big idea practically out of thin air. Get your hands on data and information related to your work and let your mind spark off it. What messages are coming through if you look hard enough? Where are the holes that can be filled? What can be used to your advantage? Three key questions to ask yourself:

1. What's missing?
2. What's frustrating?
3. What if...?

Sure, sometimes great ideas seem to come from nothing and don't apparently involve examining data. But if you dig deeper, you often find that the creator's brain was actually playing with info she'd been exposed to. Sara Blakely, the creator of Spanx, reportedly came up with the fantastic name for her company while sitting in traffic one day, but it wasn't really out of the blue. She'd already done plenty of research on brand names and had learned that the two most recognized brand names in the world, Coca-Cola and Kodak, contained a strong *k* sound, and that thought was bouncing around in her brain. She'd also read that constructed names were more successful than others, so Spanks became Spanx.

Being a mercenary for information is one of the ways Nancy Ahlum has remained the leading real estate broker (out of 2,300) in Pennsylvania's Lehigh Valley for the past ten years.

Recently Ahlum had a particular challenge on her hands. She'd been asked to try to sell a home that had been listed on and off for six years. The property was stunning, sitting on the corner of a lovely rural road, but it was fairly unique and needed a very particular kind of buyer. The bigger problem was that the previous agent had failed to unlist the property during the "off" times, so it appeared as if it had been on the market for the entire six years, suggesting (erroneously) that something was dreadfully wrong with it.

When Ahlum takes on a property, her MO is to start by combing through all the available data. Then she steps back and tries to see it from another angle. "I think it's really important to give yourself permission to look at information differently," she says. "Then ask yourself what spin you can put on it."

As Ahlum pored over the data about the property, one key thing jumped out at her. When the current owners had completed renovations on the property and added an additional entrance from the other road, they'd changed the address.

Bingo! Ahlum decided to immediately list the house under its original address, which had never appeared in any listings. The property sold within several months.

One of the best types of information to tap into when you're trying to generate ideas for products or services is the frustration faced by your customers and/or clients. Listen. Listen hard. Pay attention to what annoys people and then go big to fix it.

This is one of the strategies that Jen Furmaniak, CEO/founder of JB Talent, used to enhance her highly successful celebrity booking company in Los Angeles. In listening to clients as she built her business, Furmaniak could tell how frustrated they became when they were waiting for updates on, for instance, whether Celebrity X would agree to be a presenter at their awards ceremony. Had JB Talent contacted the celebrity's publicist yet? Had that publicist approached the celebrity? Was the celebrity even considering it? Was there a possible backup? Sometimes waiting drove them nuts.

"After realizing how frustrating this was for clients, I decided to do something really bold and go for transparency," says

Furmaniak. "I devised a system in which we create digital data cards for every celebrity we're approaching and then generate detailed reports to show who we've spoken to, who's had to pass because of other commitments, and so on. It's been so successful that now we allow our clients to access the information live through a secure portal, and they don't have to wait around for updates from us. They're part of the process."

Information gathering should be an essential part of what you do. The more information you have, the more big ideas will be sparked—as long as you practice the habit of stepping back to see everything from a fresh angle.

Two Signs You're Gun-Shy about Going Big

If you hear yourself making either of these comments about another person's big ideas, you're being defensive about not having offered up any yourself:

"I can't believe they let her get away with that."

"I would have done that, but I didn't think you were supposed to."

Go Big in Little Ways, Too.

Sometimes you need a REALLY big idea. But you can also go big in little ways, in both your job and your career. Get in the habit of stepping back from everything you do and asking yourself: **"Is there a better, bigger, bolder, or even badass way to do this?"**

Some examples:

- Just because the company you're applying to is asking for résumés to be sent digitally doesn't mean you have to stick to just that. Terri Wein, cofounder and partner of both Jobtreks and Weil & Wein, a national career advisory and executive coaching firm, says that applying for a job from an online posting should be a two-punch approach. "First, submit your résumé as instructed. Second, reach out to someone from the company via LinkedIn to avoid the black hole and introduce yourself directly."
- Just because your boss told you to "simply proofread the report" doesn't mean you can't add a top sheet with some additional info you've put together that she may find really beneficial.
- Just because your predecessor in the job always held the morning meeting in the energy-sucking conference room doesn't mean you can't hold it in your office or an area with everyone standing up. And with a box of Krispy Kreme doughnuts!
- Just because there's a podium where you're supposed to speak doesn't mean you have to stand behind it. Wouldn't your speech be more dynamic if you instead spoke out in front using a lavalier microphone?

Beware of Go-Big Wet Blankets

When you go big, almost invariably there will be people who wish you went home instead. They may feel threatened by the fact that you've come up with something totally dazzling and wouldn't mind seeing you fail, or they're sticks-in-the-mud who simply don't *get* it. To prevent those types from holding you back:

- **Don't share or "test out" your go-big idea with peers you don't totally trust before you offer them to your boss.**
- **Once your idea is out there, ignore comments like, "We tried that before but it didn't work."** That kind of remark generally is translation for, "I hate the fact that you have big ideas and I don't."
- **If people report to you, you'll want them to embrace the idea once it's ready to launch, but you don't need their approval.** If you have senior staffers you trust, by all means hear them out, but bear in mind that any negative or lukewarm reactions may simply reflect a fear of disruption.

    When I decided to change the format of *Cosmo* from a very traditional magazine—one with a bunch of unrelated articles clustered in the middle—to a format where all features and articles in the same category ran together, I excitedly told my staff. People looked at me as if I'd announced that Godzilla had just made landfall at the base of Manhattan. I wondered briefly if it wasn't a smart idea after all, but then realized it was simply the notion of change that was making them nervous. I went ahead, and newsstand sales spiked considerably after that. Readers loved that the magazine was so much easier to move through.

- **Resist gravitational pull.** When you have a really big idea, people will sometimes try to tug you (perhaps gently) away from it, and not necessarily maliciously. When chef Fernanda White decided to open a restaurant with her husband, Jake, also an acclaimed chef, they wanted the kitchen to not only be in the front of the restaurant but also in the *window*. "As chefs, we'd spent so much time in either a basement and/or back room, and we loved the idea of being out front," says White. "We knew customers would find it exciting and so would people passing by. But when the architect we shared our vision with showed us the first set of plans, he'd put the kitchen in the rear. He said it was going to be tricky and expensive to have the fans and exhaust and everything related to the kitchen right out front. But Jake and I kept coming back to the concept we'd dreamed up and written down on a napkin. And we made the architect understand that we didn't want anything else."

She believes the success of Comedor, their amazing restaurant (featuring American Chilean cuisine) in Newton, Massachusetts, is due in part to the fact that people love watching all the kitchen excitement—whether they're in the restaurant or peering in from the street.

How to Break the Rules and Not Get Spanked

If you start playing loose with the rules—and I hope you do—you may worry you could end up being called on the carpet for it. In my career, I've had certain big ideas questioned by bosses, but none ever landed me in serious hot water, and most advanced my career.

- **Establish a track record of competence.** You'll probably be more likely to have maverick ideas accepted if you've already proven you can handle the basics of your job. And bosses expect that top performers will have some big ideas that fail.

- **Be one of your boss's favorites.** She'll give you more leeway with big ideas.
- **Know the landscape.** Barbara Mikulski, the retired senator from Maryland and the longest serving woman in Congress, once told me: "You can't push the envelope until you know how the post office works."
- **If your idea is really out of the box, offer your boss two options.** Give him what he asked for and present another idea as a "fresh-take option."
- **If you do have to beg forgiveness one day, listen to your boss's criticism.** Determine what she had an issue with. Ask if she'd be open to the idea with modifications.

When They Just Won't Let You Break the Rules

Let's say that your go-big ideas are always rejected. First ask yourself if they are actually right for your department and company or if they're too self-serving. If you think they're appropriate, you're working for someone shortsighted who will probably always stifle you.

My advice: Polish your résumé and move on to a work environment that rewards breakthrough ideas. That's where your gutsy girl career will really thrive.

Now, Be a Rule Breaker Forever

I'm frequently asked for career advice by the wonderful men and women I'm lucky enough to mentor, as well as by people, referred by friends, who are facing challenges. You know who turns up for guidance more and more these days? Women in their late forties and fifties who feel suddenly unsettled. Their company or field may be going through changes, including downsizing, and these women sense they're vulnerable because of their larger salaries. And guess what? THEY ARE.

In discussing their situations with them, I often see that they've stopped going big and breaking the rules. They're resting on their laurels or relying on their subordinates to go big.

Don't make that mistake. Use the four B's every day! Show that you can still disrupt and break the rules with the best of them.

Key Gutsy Girl Takeaways

- Ask the four B's about every idea or project: Could it be better, bigger, bolder, or more badass? Use this tool in every decade of your career.
- Beware of wet-blanket people who try to water down your bold ideas or discourage them altogether.
- If you're a leader, allow your subordinates to see what a big bold idea could mean for them (their jobs and careers!) so they'll embrace it. But you don't need consensus.
- Never stop being a rule breaker.

CHAPTER 2

A Gutsy Girl Decides What She Wants to Be Famous For—and Goes After It Fearlessly

Just after I left my job running *Cosmopolitan* in 2012, I sat down for coffee with two young former NBC producers named Carly Zakin and Danielle Weisberg. They had recently started a digital newsletter for millennials called theSkimm. It featured easily digestible news items, written in a cheeky, conversational tone, that would allow young subscribers to feel in the know without having to spend a lot of time watching or reading traditional media. They'd asked for the meeting so they could pick my brain for any insights I had about young female consumers.

I was so impressed by Carly and Danielle that day, but even more so *now*. TheSkimm is a big success, with more than 5 million subscribers (80 percent women in their twenties and thirties) and currently offering other services besides the newsletter. What I particularly respect is that Carly and Danielle knew exactly what they wanted to be famous for and have owned it every step of the way. They created a clear, compelling brand that women related to instantly. Their tagline/brand statement said it all: "theSkimm makes it easier to be smarter. We read, you Skimm."

But just as theSkimm has a clear brand identity, so do Carly and Danielle personally. They're smart, gutsy entrepreneurs with a passion for news and a desire to keep young people informed.

I'm sure you've read or heard about how important it is to develop your own professional brand identity. I first learned of this concept about twenty years ago in a fantastic piece by Tom Peters titled "The Brand Called You" in *Fast Company* magazine.

Some career strategies become obsolete or downright silly-sounding over time (like, "When you're interviewing someone for a job, ask where he or she sees herself in five years," or "Always wear pantyhose to a job interview"), but Peters's advice is as sound today as it was then: *You can't move up if you don't stand out.*

Or as a business owner friend of mine says, "You have to pick a lane." Of course, several passions could weave together to create a single lane. "I love art *and* doing surgery," says Ellen Marmur, MD and president/founder of Marmur Medical. "I found my career in dermatologic surgery."

As a gutsy girl, you need to figure out what you want to be famous for and how you intend to stand out. It's not necessarily about becoming famous with a capital *F* but rather simply determining your areas of expertise, the type of work you'll find exciting, challenging, and fulfilling—and that you're either damn good at or intend to be. Your area of emphasis might easily shift over time, but you need to decide what to focus on right now, and for the period of time you can see in the car headlights. This well help shape your brand identity.

Take a moment to Google yourself. Does anything turn up? And if it does—such as your LinkedIn or social media profiles or references to you in trade publications—is it both consistent and compelling, reflecting a clear professional identity? Glance at your résumé. Could someone who sees it quickly sum up your brand?

If you answered no to those questions, it's time to decide what your brand is going to be and begin to make smart choices that will enhance it and promote it to the world.

How to Define Your Brand in Three Easy Steps

It may seem daunting to figure out what your brand is, especially if you're just launching your career, but I'm going to give you simple steps for doing it. And remember, you're not locked into anything. It can evolve or totally change over time.

The first step? Make a list, says Harper Hagedorn, global brand strategist for BMW Group. The list should be of your key assets or distinctions, or what Tom Peters called "feature benefits." These assets or benefits should reflect what you're passionate about and what you excel at (even if that's a work in progress). Aim for between seven and ten words.

When you compose your list, Hagedorn advises that you be as authentic as possible. "Just *flow*," she says. "Dig deep and understand your own self, because only then can you turn that inside out and share it with others. Embrace the quirks, the jagged, the unperfect. And learn what makes you the most *you*. Don't force it."

She points out that powerful, successful brands in the marketplace "spend millions trying to figure out authenticity and craft connection. That's the basis for brand magic, which converts consumption into obsession. It cannot be made up."

If you're right out of college or in an internship or training program, you may feel stumped for words, not sure if you have any real assets or benefits yet. Focus, then, on what you hope to be, what strengths and skills you're busy acquiring. What do you love doing most? When do you feel most in the zone? What tasks give you the most satisfaction and thrill?

According to Letena Lindsay, founder and president of L2 Public Relations, one helpful tool as you self-assess is to "ask yourself what people compliment you on and what would they miss about your performance if you left your current job."

It can also be beneficial to point-blank ask people you know what words they would use to describe your brand. "When you ask people you've interacted with professionally, you'll often hear the same words," says Nancy Berland, president of Nancy Berland Public Relations, who has helped shape the careers of mega-successful romance authors such as Lisa Jackson and Debbie Macomber. "It will give you a strong sense of what others see as your talents and assets."

Of course, if none of this feedback squares with your *own* perception of yourself, it's time for some serious assessing on your part. How do you *want* to be perceived? What are the possible reasons that you're not coming across that way? Spend time figuring it out.

If you have no clue what you want to do or what your brand should be, I'm a big believer in not sitting around with a legal pad and pen, trying to figure it out. Instead, go out into the world, be a mercenary for information, talk to people, pick their brains, try new experiences, volunteer, and the eureka moment will come.

Once you have your list, study it and narrow it down to a shorter list with only a few key assets. I happen to be partial to the idea of *three* assets. That's probably because when I took over *Cosmo*, it had one of the most powerful brand statements/ identities in publishing: **Fun Fearless Female**. Those three words captured both the reader and the magazine perfectly.

Once you have your words, form them into a statement, a kind of bumper sticker for your brand. When you're networking or interviewing, you can use this as a starting point for how you present yourself.

And if you have your own company or are planning to launch it, you need to do this very carefully for your business, too, making certain that both brand statements reflect and complement each other.

The Branding Workshop

Here's a chart that will make it easier to craft your brand statement. As I said, you start with your bigger list (seven to ten assets), pare the list to three or four, and then create a tight, compelling brand statement.

I crafted a brand statement for my current speaking career using this technique. My initial list included seven points that seemed to fit with me as a speaker: former editor in chief; bestselling author; career expert/authority; entrepreneur; advocate for gutsiness (going bigger, better, bolder); champion for women; mentor. Then I narrowed it down to three points that seemed to sum up my expertise and had a certain specificity that might be good for the speakers' market: authority; career; and bigger/ better/bolder.

From there it was easy to come up with a brand statement: Kate White is the authority on bigger, better, bolder careers.

Now, your turn.

Define Your Brand

Core Brand Assets

1. _____
2. _____
3. _____
4. _____
5. _____
6. _____
7. _____
8. _____
9. _____
10. _____

Best Three Words

1. _____
2. _____
3. _____

Brand Statement

_____

_____

_____

Next, Step Back and Assess

You've nailed your brand statement, so it's time to hold it up to several key questions:

- Does it feel true to you?
- Is it something you're really passionate about?
- Is it unique and specific enough?

The great brands offer something no one else does. And they don't try to be all things to all people. You need to pick a lane but not one that's crowded with people. Is your brand identity distinctive enough? Resist the good girl urge to want to be good at *everything*.

If your brand doesn't feel distinctive enough, consider how you might focus more tightly to give it a unique edge. In fact, it pays to consider what you will be BAD at. When I participated in the Women's Leadership Forum at Harvard Business School Executive Education program, I heard a terrific lecture by Professor Frances Frei about the importance of that concept. Frei, the author of *Uncommon Service: How to Win by Putting Customers at the Core of Your Business*, stresses that great companies decide what they're going to be bad at and then *be* bad at it, because if they try to be good at everything, there won't be enough resources to be fantastic at one important thing.

Think for a minute about theSkimm. It's a newsletter with short daily news items but it's not for everyone. It's too abbreviated, for instance, to appeal to certain news junkie baby boomers. And the cheeky tone is perfectly suited for women in their twenties and thirties.

So decide what you're going to let go of. Then ask yourself:

- **Is it viable?** Yes, you want to be true to yourself, but you also must be certain that there's a need for your brand in the marketplace (unless you have a trust fund and plan to live off that). As a successful entrepreneur once told me, it's not enough to consider what you want from the world. You have to think about what the world might want from *you*. What level of financial success are you looking for? Should you better align your professional brand with that goal?

- **Could your brand be better, bigger, bolder, or more badass?** Go through the four B's with your brand. Jeetendr Sehdev, author *The Kim Kardashian Principle*, stresses that brands that want to break through must "find their distinguishing characteristic and *amp* it up." Is your professional brand as strong and fresh as it could be? If not, how could you make it more so?

How to Mean Business with Your Brand

Now that you've defined your brand, you must own it and be ruthless about promoting it.

"One mistake I see women making is not taking their brand seriously enough," says Jen Furmaniak of JB Talent. "For instance, they start their own business, but still use their old Yahoo! address. If you're launching your own company, for instance, you need to come up with a great name, a URL, an identity. As soon as I decided to start my own business, I came up with a strong name for it. Because I knew if someone had a choice between hiring a freelance talent booker named Jen or a company called JB Talent, they'd obviously go with the latter."

Thirteen Things That Must Absolutely Reflect Your Brand

1. Your business card. Do the colors, typeface, and design look professional and reflect your key assets?
2. Your stationery. Same as above.
3. Your résumé. Often, people don't read résumés; they scan them. Weed out (without being deceptive) experiences that don't reflect your brand identity, and be sure your key brand words pop up frequently, like SEO terms, so that when someone's skimming, they lock into what's critical. (Some companies even use software to search résumés for specific words related to the job.)
4. Your cover letters. Your key words need to pop up here, too, though they must be balanced with content about what you'd like to bring to the company you're applying to. Cover letters can't be all about YOU.
5. Your digital presence. If you want to be taken seriously as a brand, every digital footprint of yours needs to be professional, smart, and reflective of your brand. I'm talking, of course, about platforms like Facebook, Twitter, and Instagram (more about these later in the chapter), but also about seemingly inconsequential stuff like your email signature. Even the tone you use in emails.
6. Your LinkedIn profile, headline, and photo. Just as with your résumé, be sure your profile uses the words you've come up with for your brand statement. And you should check for grammatical mistakes and typos as ruthlessly here as you do in your résumé and cover letters.

7. Your website. With so many easy-to-build options out there like Squarespace and Wix.com, there is no excuse for not investing in a Web presence. Everything from the color palette to the logo needs to be consistent with your "look" in other areas.

8. Your workspace. Consider every poster, card, and photo you're displaying and ask if it says the right thing.

9. Your handouts/promotional materials. Be consistent!

10. Your presentation skills. Your tone and style need to match your brand!

11. Your wardrobe. Don't skimp. If you're on a tight budget, opt for less as long as what you choose is polished and nails your brand.

12. Your hair and makeup.

13. Your purse and/or tote bag.

Of course, if you're starting your own company, everything on the list above needs to reflect the company brand identity.

Now, Build Your Brand Brilliantly

Having clearly defined your brand won't alone make you a success. You have to fully embrace it, work it, grow it, and turbocharge it whenever possible.

- When you pursue opportunities in your current job, aim to take on as many assignments as possible that will enhance your professional identity and your reputation as an employee with specific and valuable expertise. These assignments (and the big ideas you generate in conjunction with them) must serve your boss's and your company's needs, but whenever possible, let them serve your needs, too.

- Think twice about accepting a promotion or posting to a new location or a new job simply because it will "round out" your experience somehow. Maybe the opportunity will be great, but be sure you're not simply trying to improve a weakness that doesn't need improving because it doesn't fit with your brand.

- Whether you're networking or interviewing for a job, speak about yourself in a way that showcases your brand. The bumper-sticker statement you created might sound awkward in a conversation, but use it to inspire the story you tell about yourself. (I always find it so compelling when a job candidate or contact crafts their career background into a short but compelling story.) When top Manhattan attorney Susan Brune meets someone in a networking setting, she doesn't simply say, "I'm a lawyer." She says, "I'm a white-collar defense lawyer. I help Wall Street and other executives navigate through government investigations. I love a good trial, but mostly I see to it that my clients never get charged." That makes *me* want to hire her even though I'm not under arrest.

- Volunteer for company committees, particularly those that will give you a chance to showcase your strengths. Work toward taking on a leadership role.

- Don't just *join* professional organizations that fit with your brand. Volunteer to be on committees in those organizations and ultimately take on a leadership role.

- Look for any way possible to enhance and promote your expertise outside your work environment (like teaching a course or workshop), but be sure your efforts align with company policy.

- Guest blog for a website on your area of expertise or write an op-ed piece or an article for a trade publication, or a piece for LinkedIn. (There's a decent chance you'll need clearance with your boss on this.)
- Comment on other blogs and get to know their creators.
- If you have your own business, you will have started a website, but make sure it's always current and fresh and that you harvest email addresses by offering a weekly or monthly newsletter.
- Volunteer to speak or be on a panel at a professional conference. (It will help if you've got a track record of attending the conference.)
- Offer yourself as an expert to sites such as HARO (Help a Reporter Out). Again, this may need boss approval.
- Use social media to enhance your brand and do nothing to distract. Be authentic. Check company policy for guidelines.
- Create an event that you host and become known for, even something like drinks or dinner in a local restaurant for women in your field.
- Find mentors who aren't just good at giving advice but who can provide specific expertise about your brand area.
- Be gutsy enough to say no to activities that don't serve any real purpose in terms of your brand.

It will probably take some time to be "known," but chip away. Even small steps, if they're the right ones, can make a difference.

"When I first moved to LA, nothing came up if you Googled me," says screenwriter Sarah Heyward, who worked as a writer and supervising producer on Lena Dunham's HBO series *Girls*. "That changed the minute I started writing for the website

HelloGiggles. Every time I wrote an article that first year, I would get dozens of new Twitter followers. And since most of my writing on *Girls* was collaborative, it was also nice to have an outlet where I was just writing exactly what I wanted to write."

Your Brand on Social Media

As I mentioned earlier, the social platforms you use should reflect your professional brand, right down to the smallest details, like your tiny bio on Facebook and your Twitter handle. This is true even if you're using social media primarily in your personal life. That's because people you work with or people you may *hope* to work with one day have access to these platforms.

The fact is that these platforms can be a positive factor for you career-wise. "Social media offers a huge professional development opportunity," say Emma Smith-Stevens, director of strategy for the Female Quotient, a company dedicated to advancing equality. "This is a way to give people a glimpse into who you are and what you stand for outside of the office walls, though you want to be careful about oversharing. People are more likely to do business with people they know, and social media helps maintain relationships with hundreds of people easily."

What's key, says Smith-Stevens, is to identify a consistent voice to use across all platforms and posts. "A cohesive account makes people feel like they have an authentic understanding of who you are. Make sure you communicate not only your current interests, but also your future aspirations. In many ways, digital accounts have replaced résumés, so show off your strengths and be proud of who you are and what you have done."

If you use social platforms to talk about aspects of your work, you should first check your company's policy about what's okay to share. If there's no policy, use common sense. You can also check out how successful people in the organization use platforms like Facebook, Twitter, Instagram, and Snapchat.

And remember, the information you post shouldn't be all about *you*. "Don't just be a pusher," says Sean Michael, senior manager of content communications for the start-up Scout RFP. "When used smartly, social media is a conversation, not a billboard for yourself. Be part of the discourse, comment on people's posts, share a great article you read, make yourself useful to other people in the same position you have in the field." Follow the people you admire as well as your dream bosses. Join Linked-In groups they belong to. Retweet posts of theirs that you find insightful.

Most of all, be CAREFUL. "Make sure that every aspect of your social media presence—from photos to picture captions to tweets—is something you would feel comfortable with anyone seeing and having access to," says Michael. "A recent article in *Harvard Business Review* was titled 'How to Separate the Personal from the Professional on Social Media,' but I don't think you can. So ask yourself, how would you feel if your boss saw a certain post or caption of yours. Or your boss's boss. Most hiring managers can and will stalk people on social media and lots of job offers have been rescinded when the managers were left with a negative impression."

Keep in mind you need to be cautious about your footprints *anywhere* online. In 2017 a Yale University dean was fired for making disparaging remarks about people on Yelp several years before.

And what if your boss wants to friend you on Facebook? "I would decide on a case-by-case basis," says Sean Michael. "Generally speaking, I think it's good to keep a healthy division between your personal and work life and therefore you shouldn't add work superiors on social media. But if social media is relevant to your job, you might want to accept. For instance, my friend works for an art PR firm and uses of a lot of her personal social media bandwidth to promote artist events. But if your boss is just being nosy, don't accept the request."

And if she asks why you said no? Executive coach Terri Wein says to simply say you prefer to keep your personal and professional lives separate.

Why Gutsy Girls Regularly Do a Brand 360

Things change so fast these days. I watched with a lump in my throat as the print magazine business began to unravel in a few short years. Sometimes a field may be doing just fine, but the skills you need to flourish in that field start to shift.

Recently I sat at dinner next to the amazing Susan Lyne, president and founding partner of BBG (Built by Girls) Ventures (her former jobs include chairman of Gilt Groupe and president of ABC Entertainment). I asked her to tell me one key piece of advice she'd give to a younger career woman. Her response? "Realize that the field you are in will change multiple times over your career and you need to be prepared for that."

It's incredibly important, therefore, to keep a vigilant eye on what is happening in your area and make certain your brand is still valid and you have to what it takes to thrive. Terri Wein advises the following:

- Keep current on skills needed to move ahead in your field.
- Even if you are not in a job search, check out job postings for similar positions to your job. Better yet, look at

postings for your *boss's* job. What skills are required of potential candidates?

- Read industry blogs.
- Check out career and job search sites specific to your industry.
- Pay attention to merger activity to understand industry trends, consolidations, and innovations. Don't get left behind.

This is also the perfect subject to discuss with your mentors in the field. Ask their opinion on industry trends and on the specific career track you're on.

And as you move along in your career, be sure you're developing *reverse* mentors, too, younger men and women who will share thoughts on trends and technology important to them. They often have their ear close to the ground. It's even key to pay attention to changing fashion trends in your field and company. You don't want to be the last woman standing in a navy blazer.

When It's Time to Change Brands

You don't have to be famous for the same thing forever. At some point you may need to change or edit your brand because of outside circumstances. Perhaps you realize your current brand doesn't have potential for growth, or you were let go and want to try something totally new, or you moved to be with your partner and your brand isn't going to work in this location. This requires coming up with a new list of feature benefits, though your former benefits can be a starting point.

When former *Good Morning America* parenting reporter Ann

Pleshette Murphy moved to London because of her husband's job, she had to reinvent. She found it extremely helpful to make a list of what she'd loved about each of her former jobs, which included years as an award-winning editor in chief of *Parents* magazine. She had also recently earned a master's degree in psychology.

"I examined everything through the filter of what I really enjoyed doing and what I found most gratifying," she says. "There had been a definite ego boost to being on *GMA*, but my inertia about finding a TV job in London told me that wasn't so important anymore. What was *most* gratifying to me, I realized, was connecting to mothers, listening to their stories, and offering them guidance. I loved hearing someone say, 'That's so helpful. I hadn't thought of that,' or 'Your advice changed our lives.' At the core for me was a desire to be a parenting educator/counselor and the freedom to work from home."

Today Murphy does private and group parenting counseling in her home and loves it.

And sometimes you may just feel ready for a change, for a chance to reinvent yourself. Or for a chance to finally start your own company.

I had that moment in my own life. As much as I loved being in the magazine business and running a brand as fantastic as *Cosmo*, I eventually came to see that I wanted to have a more entrepreneurial work life with total control over my schedule. While still at *Cosmo*, I began writing murder mysteries and thrillers with an eye to a future that would involve writing books and public speaking. Nowadays that's called having a side hustle, but back then I thought of it as Plan B (it was also a safety net in case I got fired!).

Some clues it may be time for a new brand called you:

- You feel bored a lot.
- You're insanely envious of what a friend or former colleague is doing.
- The marketplace has become too crowded with people with a similar brand.

Go ahead. Give yourself permission to change brands.

Key Gutsy Girl Takeaways

- Define your brand by listing seven to ten characteristics, boiling those down to three or four, and then shaping that into a sentence.
- Make everything reflect your brand. From your website to your shoes!
- Don't be afraid to be really bad at something.
- Remember, you don't have to be famous for the same thing forever.

CHAPTER 3

A Gutsy Girl Knows How to Hustle

So far I've talked about the importance of knowing what you want to be famous for, as well as going really big and badass with your ideas. Now it's time to discuss getting busy—but busy in a *smart*, gutsy way.

A gutsy girl knows how to *hustle*, focus on the essential goal, move quickly toward it, look for unexpected openings, and not be overly worried if some things are a little rough around the edges or if certain tasks get left behind for someone else to handle—or simply get left behind *period* because, in the end, they're not really required.

Hustling is what helps you achieve your goals.

Good girls tend not to be hustlers. They wait around to be told what to do, get bogged down in paper-pushing tasks they shouldn't be spending nearly as much time on (or maybe shouldn't be bothering with at all), and work at perfecting things to a fault, worried that if they move too fast, they'll miss a step or screw up. And they say yes to everything they're asked to do.

"There's something very seductive about being a 'yes' girl," says time management and productivity expert Julie Morgenstern. "You're trying to show you're indispensable, not only to your boss but perhaps also to people from other departments who need a hand. But if you get caught in this kind of good girl mentality and define your value primarily in terms of volume, it will detract from your core value and you won't have time to do what you're best at."

If your good girl tendencies have left you in the weeds, it's time to machete your way out and start hustling. You must determine what's essential to you, tackle those essentials like a house on fire, and not give a rat's ass about the rest.

Figure Out What Matters—and What Should Be Dumped or Ignored

You're probably in the habit of starting a task or project with a to-do list, because hey, to-do lists work. You consider your objective and then figure out the necessary steps. But don't believe everything on your to-do list. There's probably stuff on there that's sucking up time and energy unnecessarily and either doesn't have to be done or could or should be done by someone else.

When Jen Furmaniak started JB Talent, she used the first part of each day to focus on the key aspect of her new business— acquiring clients. She then devoted the hours between 3:00 p.m. and 6:00 p.m. to handling bookkeeping responsibilities. She disliked those tasks, but they had to be done. And since she was a one-person operation, there was no one to delegate to.

But one day Furmaniak finally stepped back and realized that she was wasting valuable time by doing the bookkeeping herself. Yes, it was essential but not essential for *her* to handle. "I discovered I could actually hire a freelance bookkeeper for $20,000 a year, which on one hand was a lot of money, but if I used the late afternoon to acquire clients, I'd be making way more than I needed to pay for a bookkeeper. It was so much smarter for me to be using my time doing what I'm best at."

Make it your business to routinely step back from what you're working on and evaluate whether those tasks are necessary for you to reach your company's goals and your own.

"What you're looking for," says Morgenstern, who is the *New York Times* bestselling author of six books, including *Organizing from the Inside Out*, "is the convergence of what you've been hired to produce and your personal brand. How do your boss and your company spell success and measure results in terms of the revenue line? Plus, what are your unique skills and talents and the things that make you truly indispensable?"

If you realize that you're not 100 percent sure of how your boss spells success at this given moment (it can shift!), schedule a time to talk to her. Say you want to touch base about what she sees as the most important goals for you to meet, right here and right now.

Think about your own objectives, too, what you want to be focusing on in terms of your professional brand. Once you've crystalized both the goals your boss has for you and those you have for yourself, use the following chart to help determine what should be on your to-do list and what shouldn't.

What's key is to ask yourself these questions every week, not just every month or year, because nonessential tasks have a way of creeping into your schedule.

Watch out, too, for the ripple effect, projects and activities that begin to appear on your to-do list as a by-product of your success and *seem* to be of value but aren't. As rewarding and ego boosting as some of them may be, they could be craftily

The Essentials Quiz

Ask yourself these questions about everything on your to-do list

Is this really what I should be doing (want to be doing) right this second?

Yes ☐   ☐ No

_____

_____

What should I be doing?

Will this activity definitely get me closer to my work goals and also help me enhance my brand?

Yes ☐   ☐ No

_____

_____

What's a better use of my time?

Is this something that I could give someone else to do?

← Yes ☐   ☐ No →

Who? _____   **Why not?** _____

Think it over a minute more.

Could this actually be delegated to a subordinate, freelancer, virtual assistant, travel agent, college student for $20/hour, Siri, or Alexa?

Yes ☐   ☐ No

Is this something that really doesn't have to be done at all?

☐ Yes   ☐ No   ☐ Gosh, I've never thought about that

_____

What's the worst that could happen if it doesn't get done?

detracting from the main mission. PR expert Nancy Berland works with amazing authors whose workdays often begin to expand with ripple activities as their success grows. "I had a terrific client who readers adored and before long she was in constant demand as a speaker," says Berland. "She sometimes had several speaking engagements a *day*, which really started to shift her focus. The question I encourage someone in that kind of situation to ask herself is, '**What is it I really want to be?**' "

The answer in this case was "author, not speaker," which forced the author to consider how much these speeches were enabling her goal. "When you're an author, a certain amount of speaking is, of course, good for exposure," says Berland. "But the very best promotion you can do is write another *book*."

Keep asking yourself: "Is this activity, exciting as it may be, getting me closer to fulfilling my goals?"

How to Say No When Necessary

To someone besides your boss, say: "I'd love to help out, [if it's a higher-up, you could say "I'm honored to be asked..."] but right now X [your boss or the company] is counting on me to deliver Y, and I wouldn't be able to do either task justice if I took on both."

To your boss, say: "I want to be sure I can do this well in the context of my other responsibilities. Can I review my immediate priorities with you first?" If possible, suggest an alternative—for instance, giving the project to someone else but having you monitor it.

Okay, Now Be a Baller

Once you fine-tune your list of essentials, you'll probably feel less stressed and more in control. But knowing the essentials and deciding to tackle them isn't enough. You want to be a *baller*. In basketball, a baller is a player who runs the floor planning to score, always looking for the open shot, and if it's not there, creates one.

One of the best ballers I've met is actress, author, and comedian Amy Schumer. I first laid eyes on Amy when she was in her early twenties and performing in a play with my husband, cast as a teenage girl, though at the time, she was doing stand-up comedy as well as acting.

I remember being total mesmerized by Amy's performance in the play (when, needless to say, I wasn't staring at my husband!). She was completely and fully engaged in the experience. The theater was a fairly small one, and her part wasn't huge, but she played it with an energy level comparable to Vivien Leigh in *Gone with the Wind*.

A few years later, wowed by Amy's comedy, I asked her to write some funny essays for me at *Cosmo*. They were terrific. Then I asked her to star in a series of videos for an app we launched called *Cosmo for Men*. We gave her very little direction but the videos were beyond hilarious.

The thing about Amy is that she is *always* all-in, always moving decisively, looking for the best shot or creating one, not waiting for directions. I invited her to a dinner party at my home once and she came dressed in this smashing dress with her hair and makeup clearly done by pros. I assumed she was probably attending another event afterward, and yet when I thought about it later, I wasn't so sure. Maybe she'd simply told herself, "You never know who I might meet at dinner tonight so let me look fantastic."

As a baller you must:

- get moving on what matters;
- bring your A game;
- look for openings that may not be readily apparent—and if there aren't any, create them;
- never wait around to be told what to do;
- avoid overthinking things;
- steer clear of tasks that don't matter.

How to Find an Opening When None Is Apparent

Sometimes when you want to hustle, you may not be able to spot a clear opportunity. You may feel blocked or stymied by circumstances. It's time, then, to find an opening or a window that may not be perfectly obvious. And if you can't find it, be gutsy and *create* one.

A huge break early in my career came from using this strategy. I was a junior writer at *Glamour* magazine, producing short pieces like "How to Get Rid of a Pimple by Saturday Night," and though it was fun, I wanted to make my mark writing big features. I pitched an idea for a major reporting piece to the editor in chief and was bluntly told that (despite my pimple research skills) I didn't have enough experience to tackle that. I spent weeks trying to figure out if there was another way to approach the situation. What I needed to do, I decided, was to write something that required no research! Though the magazine didn't run essays, I decided to try that route. I wrote a full-length, first-person feature (without asking permission) about being single in New York City. The editor loved it, and though it was never optioned for a TV series that would star Sarah Jessica Parker, the article received an unprecedented amount of mail and I was told to keep the essays coming. I soon had my own column.

At times you may want to work at creating several potential openings at the same time and see what comes through first. "Instead of having a linear game plan, I have always had multiple plans in play," says Dr. Ellen Marmur. "For example, starting my own practice was actually Plan B, not Plan A. I wanted to stay in my current position [at a medical hospital], but I knew that once I began negotiating some key changes, I risked losing my job. I even had a third option in play, to work for another institution, before I took my big risk. Like any chess game, you should always try to forecast multiple strategies and when the other person makes their decision, you move swiftly from any of your vantage points."

The Sneaky Trick That Will Help Get Your Butt Moving

Here's a great little secret about people who hustle and get things done. They don't always start at the *beginning*, and that gives them a critical advantage. Yes, it's essential to do your homework when necessary, but don't do it to death, and stop worrying you'll be fined if you skip a few early steps that are considered obligatory (please ignore this pointer if you work in medicine or for NASA, though!). Sometimes jumping ahead will move you toward your objective more quickly, and it will totally energize you as well.

That's what Jen Glantz did when she was toying with the concept for her business, BridesmaidforHire.com. Jen had been a bridesmaid in a ton of weddings. She had mounds of chiffon dresses stuffed in her closet and had watched way more than her share of guys in thongs twerk too close to her face at bachelorette parties. During these experiences she'd begun to notice a gap in the billion-dollar bridal marketplace. On the day of the wedding, the planner would be handling final logistical details and the bridesmaids would be getting dressed, which meant there was no one around to help the bride. Jen began to toy with the idea of creating a business to serve the last-minute needs of a bride.

Now, some of the usual first steps recommended for starting your own business include asking people for their opinions and writing up a business plan, but Jen decided to just completely skip those.

"I knew if I told anyone that I wanted to hire myself out as a professional bridesmaid, they might discourage me," she says, "so I didn't say a word and I tried not to think too much about it.

"Instead I went straight to Craigslist and tested the idea. I asked women if they'd want a service like this and I got 250 emails in reply! From there I organized the emails into buckets based on the exact things people were looking for, and I used those buckets to create the packages I offered on my website."

Sometimes you have to skip over steps because that's the only way to find an opening.

Five Reasons You May Be Stuck

As determined as you may be to act like a baller and get down to business, you might end up stalled or even stuck in the mud. You sit on a project or report, avoid making necessary calls, or put off a major decision. Consider these possible explanations for your paralysis and then act on them.

1. **You've made the task too ginormous.** One of the best strategies a productivity expert ever taught me was to "slice

the salami" with projects. Break an overwhelming project down into small steps. How small? As small as necessary to make each step so easy it practically completes itself. When I began writing my first murder mystery, I was worried about my ability to stick to the task, so I wrote for only fifteen minutes a day for the first six months.

2. **You don't have enough information.** Trendera CEO Jane Buckingham says that when the information you're looking at confuses you about what course to follow, obtain *more* information to help clarify the matter. Let's say you've just taken over a department and a critical goal for you right now is building your own team. But the process is moving more slowly than it should and you're having trouble deciding on candidates. So *reinterview* your candidates with a new set of questions or give them a test assignment. Learning even more about each individual will help you decide.

3. **You have too much on your plate and aren't delegating stuff.** (See How to Delegate Unapologetically, page 55)

4. **You're waiting for your boss to provide more insight or even give you the go-ahead.** In an ideal world, your boss will hand you terrific assignments and clear guidelines, but that doesn't always happen. He may not realize that you're waiting for more info or even that you want to be assigned a particular task to begin with. ASK.

5. **You're trying too hard to make it perfect.** I'd never suggest that your work should be sloppy or incomplete (that's a no-no), but if you're too much of a good girl perfectionist, your ideas will grow stale and soggy and you may never launch them. To say nothing of how annoyed your boss will be if you're dragging your heels.

If you hear yourself uttering any of the following phrases, it's a sign you're trying too hard to be perfect:

"I'm just putting the finishing touches on it."

"I want to get it right."

"I have to iron out all the wrinkles."

"This is going to be *really* comprehensive."

So let *go*. "Don't overthink it," says Sarah Friar, CFO of Square, the mobile payment company. "Get it out there and see if it resonates. Often what you planned to create isn't what you end up with because interacting with customers lets you gain insight and rethink quickly. It's through imperfection that you often learn the most."

In most cases you can generally massage an idea or project, making it stronger, once you put it out there and gather feedback.

Six Butt-Saving Time Management Strategies

1. **Be the boss of your time.** Make it conform to your needs, not the other way around.
2. **Schedule anything that matters on your calendar,** rather than simply telling yourself you'll find time as the week goes along. Be sure to include chunks of time for drumming up big ideas.
3. **Never waste your time (or someone else's) by saying, "I'll get back to you on that."** Learn to make instant decisions.
4. **Never handle a piece of paper (or email) more than once.**
5. **Limit social media and email to certain times of day.** It's best to avoid constantly switching back and forth between these and other tasks. "It takes four times longer for your

brain to recognize each task it's working on when you're switching back and forth," says Morgenstern. Switching costs you time, energy, and brainpower.

6. **Set boundaries.** No one will do it for you. If people are constantly stopping by your cube to gab, for instance, learn to say, "I need to focus on my project for the next two hours. What if we grab coffee at 11:30?"

How to Delegate Unapologetically

If you have people reporting to you, don't make the good girl mistake of assuming some of their responsibilities. *Delegate.*

- **Rather than ask someone to do something, instruct him to do it.** And be as clear as possible. Say, "Please order fifteen copies of this. I'll need them by 4:00 p.m. today."
- **If the task is complicated, go by the "rule of three."** That's advice from Julie Morgenstern. "When I'm delegating, I like to tell people, 'When this comes back, I'll be looking for the following,' and then I tell them the three most important objectives. That helps them focus."
- **Don't overexplain or launch into the reasons you can't do it yourself.**
- **When applicable, point out the value of the task to the person you're delegating to.** For instance, "I want you to take the meeting in my place. It will be a great chance for you to meet the people in sales."
- **Trust people to do what you've told them to do.** "I was so hesitant to take a vacation," says chef and restaurant owner

Fernanda White, "but once I finally did it, I returned and discovered everything had gone perfectly when I was away. I had a staff I trusted. I'd shown them the ropes, so I shouldn't have been surprised."

- **Never let subordinates delegate to *you*.** When you're a manager, your staff will be tempted to unload problems on you and expect you to solve them. A famous and much shared *Harvard Business Review* article defined this as "passing the monkey." When a subordinate tries to pass the monkey to you, insist that he or she figure out the correct solution to be implemented and share that with you for your approval.

Special Hustle Tips for Interns

Even if you don't hope to work for the company (or even in the same field) one day, you should be viewing your internship as an opportunity to make contacts, find mentors, and gain invaluable experience. Over the years I've worked with some fabulous interns, several of whom I'm still in contact with, but also with interns who've been lazy and immature and blew a great opportunity. Bring your A game every day.

Win Friends and Influence People

When you're moving fast in your job and your career, generating big ideas and executing them brilliantly, you may fail to notice the impact your hustling has on those around you. You may inadvertently step on toes or threaten people simply by your bravo performance.

You really want to avoid that. It's critical to develop and foster good relationships with your coworkers. Not only will this make work more rewarding for you on a personal level (and for your coworkers, too), but it helps guarantee success.

Midway through my career, a common piece of job wisdom I often heard from experts was that it didn't matter if people liked you; what you needed instead was for people to simply respect you. But I don't buy that. I think that being liked can be a huge advantage in your career.

Of course, not everyone is going to like you and you should never turn into an obsequious people pleaser. You should never base your decisions on how much people will like you. If your cheeks are sore from smiling all day, and your neck aches from nodding, you're suffering from the disease to please. But the more people you win to your side, the more effective you will be. To say nothing of the fact that work is a great place to develop lifelong friendships and, yes, even romances.

Here are some basic strategies.

Your boss: Work hard at having a great rapport with your boss. Ben Dattner, PhD, a New York City–based executive coach and organizational psychologist, as well the author of *Credit and Blame at Work*, says he sometimes tells clients that they have only three priorities in their jobs: "(1) Make your boss look good; (2) make your boss *feel* good; (3) do well at your actual job."

Theoretically your boss is supposed to manage the relationship, but don't leave it all to him. Determine how your boss prefers to be communicated with, including his face-time factor (how much is too much and how little is too little), and whether email is preferred over phone calls or popping by his desk. Ask for clear deadlines and meet them. Take notes when he hands you an assignment. Pay attention to common phrases he uses and consider what they reveal about his priorities. Compliment his ideas. Ask for feedback. Accept criticism (see The Gutsy Girl's Guide to Accepting Criticism, page 131). Ask for more projects to handle. Offer to help when the heat is on. Praise him to higher-ups when you're chatting at events. Be enjoyable to manage. And sometimes kiss butt.

This is especially important when your boss changes. Don't assume your job is secure. Demonstrate you're on your new boss's team, invested in her agenda, and willing to help each step of the way.

Of course, what matters most is to perform fabulously. Does your boss pay you compliments, give you choice assignments, and invite you to important meetings? As I mentioned earlier, have you made him say "Wow" lately? If not, don't plant a negative by asking, "Is something wrong?" Schedule a time to talk and review the goals your boss has for you. Make sure you're delivering more than 100 percent and generating go-big ideas.

Remember that though you're building your own professional brand, your actions must always advance the company goals and make your boss look like a rock star. That's how you end up being viewed as totally *indispensable*.

Your coworkers: Having good relationships with your peers, both in your own department and in other departments, not only helps make work more personally gratifying and fun, it also inspires peers to become allies who can foster your success while you foster theirs. So be good to your peers. Share information. Listen and ask questions. Support their ideas in meetings. Follow through on what you promise to do for them. Carry your weight on teams and committees. Don't humble-brag to them about your successes. Don't bad-mouth them to others. Don't betray their confidences. Stay in touch when they move on because they can be great contacts.

"As diverse as many of us believe we are, the reality is that most of us have more things in common than not," says Marie Perry, EVP, Chief Financial Officer and Administration Officer at Jamba Juice. "I have found that the best way to build relationships and alliances with your peers is by finding the common connections you share. I strive to identify new opportunities to connect with my colleagues each day, whether that be stopping to talk on my way to grab something off the printer or on the way to a meeting."

I sometimes hear women talk these days about the importance of having a work wife, a woman who has your back and vice versa. What a good idea. If there's a woman (or women) you really connect with, slowly test the waters and see if you can count on her as a sounding board, someone to run ideas by, and swap pertinent info with.

Last, but certainly not least, be considerate to those below you in the hierarchy. They can be valuable allies, too. Besides, if you are rude to them as you hustle to make your mark, they might find ways to undermine you, such as gossiping about you or not providing you with info you need.

Men in particular: I've had some great male bosses and many great male colleagues, and several of my closest friends are guys I once worked with. It's not something I really overthought. In fact, that's probably the best way to approach men at work. "If you're focusing on differences between men and women, you miss out on finding great thought partners," says Ana Marshall, vice president and chief investment officer for the Hewlett Foundation.

But let's face it, interacting with *certain* guys on the job offers a challenge. Some have big egos and thin skins, and gutsy girls can be threatening to them. These guys sometimes turn into work jerks—people who box you out, refuse to share info, dismiss your ideas in meetings (and then later co-opt a version of those ideas for themselves), and often try to outmaneuver you.

It can be even more complicated when you work in a male-dominated setting and are totally outnumbered. Guys in these situations often seem to develop a pack mentality and power in numbers. Research shows, for instance, a woman is more likely to be interrupted by a guy in a meeting if there are mostly men at the table.

Take preventive measures by working to turn potentially difficult male coworkers into allies. Two strategies:

1. **Let them see your funny side.** That helps humanize you to guys who are easily threatened. "Having a sense of humor is more than being able to laugh about a situation later with friends," says Alexandra Lebenthal, who, as CEO of Lebenthal & Co (an investment services company focusing on municipal bonds), has worked on Wall Street for years. "It is being able to deal with men at work by actively using and expressing that sense of humor." You don't have to be a joke teller. Rather, share a laugh over something crazy that happened on *Game of Thrones*. Or if

he worships his golden retriever, send him a link to a funny BuzzFeed post about dogs.

2. **Divide and conquer.** Invite a guy to coffee or lunch. Ask him about himself and his family. He'll be far less likely to diss your idea at a meeting if he's started to think of you as a work pal.

Some of this people navigating falls under the umbrella of "office politics," strategies used at work to give you an advantage. A certain amount of politics is necessary but there's no fun in getting mired in it, especially the ugly kind. In addition to being smart about how you deal with people, you can avoid toxic politics by working for a sane boss who eschews office drama. And/ or choosing a certain type of job. "Politics can mean sucking up, figuring out what's important to someone so you can deliver it, kissing the ring, and, the higher up you go, betting on the right horse," says my friend in equities. "But performance-based jobs mean you don't have to be so political. Everything's there in black and white."

Sarah Friar echoes that sentiment. "A female mentor used to say that in a male-dominated business, it can be smart to gravitate toward areas that can be quantified. For instance, if you trade stocks, you are graded every day on the results. Then it doesn't matter if you were left out the conversation on the golf course when the boy's club kicked into gear."

Be a Baller with Your Career, Too

If it's early in your career, you'll want to focus as much as possible on mastering your job, but it's also important to pay attention to your brand and your career, keeping an eye on where you're headed and not allowing for continental drift. In the beginning you may not have a clear idea of exactly what you hope to achieve, and that's okay, but you want to be proactive.

- **Take your pulse regularly.** Do you like what you're doing? Does it fit with your overall goals for yourself and your values? If you're not sure, talk to people in other fields, pick their brains, and set up exploratory interviews (using contacts, friends, and LinkedIn to help you make connections).

  More than satisfied in your field? Still check your pulse regularly. If you've been in a job for two to four years, it's important to ask yourself if it's time to move and stretch. Being really, really happy in a position is often the first hint you're ready for new challenges.

- **Strengthen your strengths.** This is advice I've always favored from Marcus Buckingham, business consultant, motivational speaker, and author of *Now, Discover Your Strengths*. He believes you move up by making your strengths even stronger. And what about your weaknesses? Buckingham advises that you not waste time trying to improve at those. Instead simply neutralize them or manage around them.

- **Never stop networking.** You shouldn't cut back because you have a job. And engage in plenty of cyber-networking, too. Join LinkedIn groups (thought leaders, professional groups) for both knowledge sharing and striking up online relationships with people you might not be able to connect with in person. If you rely on LinkedIn to hear about job openings in your field (use the menu to list your criteria), you'll be able to discover who among your first-degree connections has contacts in a particular company and can be asked for email intros where appropriate. And cyber-networking also means staying in touch online with key contacts. Send them short updates about your career and links to articles and/or events they may find worthwhile so you aren't always simply going to them for an "ask." And when people do help you, send a thank-you note. Please!

- **If you haven't done so already, begin developing mentors/ sponsors.** "Mentors enlarge your professional network and keep you grounded in those inevitable moments when you want to change jobs because you are running from some-thing," says Ana Marshall. "A great mentor listens and pulls you down to realizing much of what you dislike will exist in all the other places you could jump to." She recommends that in the first decade of your career, you find a mentor outside the firm who is "vested in your career, has a broad network of people, and helps you think of the possibilities before you." For your second decade, she recommends a new outside mentor who has a *deep* network of contacts to help you broaden your own network. She also recommends that as your career develops, you find one internal mentor/ sponsor, a senior partner or executive who has no direct oversight of the area you work in but knows the firm enough to provide insight.

- **Don't simply ask a mentor for advice. Ask him/her to open doors for you as your sponsor.** And again, send a thank-you note for any help you receive!

And if your company has a mentoring program, take advantage. In his research David Thomas, H. Naylor Fitzhugh Professor of Business Administration at Harvard

Business School, found that white male executives often feel uncomfortable reaching out directly to young women to mentor them, yet they're eager to mentor assigned protégés.

- **Be a brain-sucking zombie when you meet successful people.** Never pass up the chance to learn from them. Ask questions like, "What's the best professional advice you've been given? What's the biggest mistake you see younger people making in the field?" and "What trends in the field excite you the most? And alarm you the most?"

The Gutsy Girl's Guide to the Side Hustle

I couldn't be more in favor of having a side hustle (which as I mentioned earlier was once known as "having a Plan B"). After all, I had two fabulous ones during my magazine career (public speaking and writing books), and both laid the foundation for me to later leave corporate life and become my own boss as a speaker and author. A side hustle helps you determine if you might want to try another career path one day, and it gives you a nice backup if things don't go as planned in your existing career.

- If you want a side hustle but don't know where to start, look for epiphany moments when you feel totally in the zone and focused.
- Don't create a fairy tale. If you hope to eventually make money with your side hustle one day, do your homework (and the math), and make sure there's a market for your idea.
- Really test the waters, perhaps in a volunteer capacity. I wrote eight murder mysteries while I was still in magazines and was dead sure, so to speak, that I wanted to go down that road.

- But don't cheat on your job. I once had a junior fashion editor who started her own line of clothing using interns and the company messenger service to assist in the launch. Not nice. Cheaters get caught and pay a price.

- Recognize when it may be time to finally go all-in. "One of the most important pieces of advice we got early on," say Carly Zakin and Danielle Weisberg, cofounders and co-CEOs of theSkimm, "was that if we expected someone to invest in our idea, we had to invest in it first. That meant quitting our jobs and risking everything for it. It's a hard pill to swallow because there are obviously huge financial implications that make it a chicken-and-egg problem, but ultimately if you are going to take investor money for your side hustle, you need to be prepared to quit your day job."

- Just know that being your own boss sometimes sucks. I fantasized about working for myself very early in my career, and I'm actually glad I didn't do it until much later. Moving up the ranks in a fantastic corporation provided me with everything from a great salary to health care to a wonderful pension plan.

Okay, Now Do One Thing That's Totally Unessential

Work and life wouldn't be much fun if you were a total slave to your to-do list and did only what's essential. Allow for spontaneity and for your brain to recharge. Some of the best ideas often occur when you're in unexpected places or just thinking.

So leave work early one day and head to the movies, say yes to lunch with someone in a totally different field, get a manicure *and* a head rub.

Key Gutsy Girl Takeaways

- Decide what's essential. Focus on that and dump the rest.
- Be a baller. Bring your A game, look for openings, and don't wait to be told what to do.
- Let go of the desire to be perfect. It will only slow you down.
- Start to form alliances even as you hustle. You will need them.
- Be a baller with your career, too.

CHAPTER 4

A Gutsy Girl Gets That Appearances Matter (Fair or Not)

During the years I was running *Cosmo*, I developed a rule that I know my entertainment editor thought was fairly insane. I refused to meet with any celebrity who I was considering putting on the cover.

Okay, I actually have a sound explanation for this crazy rule. Within my first year at the magazine, I discovered that I had a pretty good knack for picking cover girls who would guarantee a great sale on the newsstand. I followed a strategy I developed (through both research and trial and error) that relied on one simple criterion: the level of curiosity and fascination I sensed readers had about a certain celebrity at that moment in time. And it had nothing to do with what the woman was like personally, how well her latest movie or album did, how many social media followers she had, or whether her naked ass could break the Internet. I knew that meeting with someone face-to-face would do nothing to illuminate me on how curious readers were about her.

But one time I made an exception. The actress really wanted to meet (clearly to lobby for a cover) and since I was a fan and thought it would be fun, I said yes. Well, she was dazzling. Great hair, great face, great style, and absolutely charming. Because I was so dazzled, I overrode my usual criterion (the curiosity factor) and ran a cover on her in part because of how she'd come across in person. It didn't do well at all.

That experience reinforced for me the degree to which impressions (first or otherwise) matter, and that fact has real implications for us in our careers. Maybe it would be nice to be judged solely on our skills and experience, but our appearance, as well as our body language, and the way we talk, greatly influences how others respond to us, often in ways that aren't even recognized by the observer on a conscious level.

Just consider this: According to research, the decision *not* to hire is frequently made within the first five to fifteen minutes of a job interview. Other research shows that people often nab a lasting first impression of us within thirty seconds. And those quick impressions are based partly on how we dress and wear our hair, how we speak, and how we carry ourselves.

Though it may not be fair, style can often count as much as substance, and sometimes even more. So let go of any good girl desire to be judged only on your merits. Having style *and* substance will give you a terrific edge. What you are really doing is just translating your gutsiness into the way you look, sound, and come across.

How a Gutsy Girl Dresses

There's been so much said about how women should dress in professional situations and it's always shifting. Today at least (compared to when I first started working), many women feel free, even within whatever confines their profession might present, to dress in a way that feels authentic to them. Be *you*, and pick clothes you love. But keep these key gutsy girl principles in mind:

- **Dress as if you mean business.** As Vanessa Friedman, fashion director at the *New York Times*, put it so succinctly, "If you want to be taken seriously, you had better think seriously about every message you are sending, including the ones in your outfits." Of course, how you show you mean business with your clothes depends on the field you're in. It could mean going with anything from polished conservative to ultra hip to hoodie casual. Check out the powerful, successful women in your professional world and let the clothes they wear be a guide.

- **Dress for the job you aspire to.** This is ancient advice but it still stands. If your goal is to one day have a job in your company that's higher up from where you are now, dress as if you're already in that job, or even beyond. Don't try to convince yourself that since subordinates aren't expected to "dress up," you don't have to do so yet. It can be hard for a boss to envision you in a new role if you're not acting the part on every level. Be warned that some of your peers may smirk or complain when you upgrade your wardrobe, but don't let their comments stop you.

- **Less is more.** Better to have a small number of quality separate pieces in neutral colors (like black and beige) that you mix and match than a lot of stuff that looks cheap.

- **When in doubt, wear stilettos—or whatever makes you feel at the top of your game.** When I dropped by my first *Cosmo* cover shoot, I was surprised to see that the model for that issue had picked out a great pair of stilettos to wear with each outfit, despite the fact that our covers almost never showed the woman's feet. My design director explained that in general, models we shot for the cover loved wearing stilettos because "all that height gives them a feeling of power."

Certain items of clothing do that, and you probably have a few in your closet already. Maybe it's not actually a pair of stilettos, but rather a particular statement necklace or a great pencil skirt. You not only feel super confident when you wear it, but you also know it works because people often compliment you. Buy as many confidence builders as possible and wear them when it matters most.

Clothes can even be used to make a specific statement. When PR executive Deb Shriver's boss was fired at one point during her career, Deb purposely wore a red dress and red lipstick to work the next day and made a point of buying her lunch in the cafeteria. "It was a way for me to show it was business as usual," she says.

- **Develop a signature look.** This will not only make it easier for you to shop, but a signature look also commands attention. That's how Megyn Kelly enhanced her image while hosting her show for Fox News. With the help of stylist Dana Perriello, Kelly developed a definitive, powerful look that Perriello described as "very polished and almost sharp." It featured tailored jackets and body-conscious dresses, with no frills or florals, similar to the look of Claire Underwood on *House of Cards*. It was feminine but also said, "Don't mess with me."

- **Make sure your hair and makeup mean business, too.**
Get a killer haircut, one that fits with your aspirations.
And have someone show you how to apply makeup so that
it looks polished. Bobbi Brown, makeup artist and former COO of Bobbi Brown Cosmetics, says it's important,
especially when applying makeup, to look like yourself, at
your best. "Wear makeup that naturally enhances your
features," she says, "and that isn't distracting or inappro-
priate for the workplace. All you really need are a skin-tone
correct concealer to brighten under your eyes, an eye-
opening mascara, a pretty pink blush that looks like your
cheeks when they are naturally flushed, and a lip gloss to
polish off the look."

Don't convince yourself it doesn't matter. It *does*. And if
there's one thing I learned from looking at a zillion photos during my magazine years, it's that you should have your eyebrows
professionally shaped by a real expert so they don't run the risk
of looking like commas, sperm, or hockey sticks. It can make a
huge difference.

Image Tips Just for Interns

The same "dress for the job you aspire to" tip applies when
you're interning, and that job is *not* "college student." Before
you start, check out the company website or ask the point
person you dealt with for guidance on dress code. If you
calculate wrong, adjust immediately for day two.

How a Gutsy Girl Speaks

When we think of how we come across, it's easy to focus mostly on appearance, but your voice and the words you use play a big part, too. Just as you must dress for the job you aspire to, Sylvia Ann Hewlett, an economist and the founder and chief executive of the Center for Talent Innovation, advises that you "*speak* for the job you aspire to."

That means unloading certain speaking habits and verbal tics that undermine your credibility. Dr. Lillian Glass, an expert on human behavior, body language, and communication, says that the most common bad habits she sees among women include:

- not enunciating enough;
- not having energy in your voice;
- up-talk (ending statements as if they were questions, as in "I'm in *advertising*?");
- constantly using fillers such as *um*, *uh*, and *you know*;
- speaking in too high of a pitch, which can suggest a lack of authority. (Glass suggests pressing down on your stomach when you speak and seeing how much lower this might make your voice.)

To determine if you've adopted any of these bad habits, use your phone to secretly tape yourself in a meeting and then listen. Make necessary adjustments. (See How to Banish Fillers, page 73.)

One of the biggest mistakes women make when speaking, says Glass, is ***failing to get to the point***. This is something good girls are particularly guilty of. Out of either nervousness or a need to show how much homework they've done (or both), they offer a ton of background info at the front end.

Homework can be important, but save that for the back end, or when your boss asks you to expand. Otherwise you'll lose listeners and appear lacking in confidence.

Don't say: "When I was at the conference, I heard some people talking about what was happening in California and then when I got back I did some research. I noticed this really interesting trend. Sales of X have grown nine percent in California. Maybe there's something we should do with that."

Instead say: "Sales of X have grown nine percent in California. That's an opportunity we should consider jumping on."

Phrases You Should Always Avoid Using

Own your ideas. Practice stating them before a meeting. When sharing, be clear, concise, and don't qualify. Never begin with the following phrases or anything resembling them.

- "Maybe we…"
- "I'm not sure, but…"
- "I kind of think…"
- "I'm just throwing this out there…" or "I'm just spitballing here…"

How to Banish Fillers

Almost everyone uses fillers at times. But it's distracting to the listener and, when overdone, can make you seem unprepared and unsure. Glass offers a trick for preventing yourself from using fillers: Take a breath after each sentence you speak. Hold for a second. Then exhale as you make your next statement. Exhaling will make it harder to use a filler.

Help, You're Being "Mansplained"

No matter how well you come across when you speak, no matter how great your expertise on a subject and your confidence in presenting, there will probably be times when a guy in the room who knows less than you do steps in and tries to explain it better, in some cases even simply repeating what *you* said. This is known these days as *mansplaining* and I think most of us have had it foisted on us.

How you handle it depends on the guy and the circumstances.

If it's someone you work with, particularly someone on your level, it probably won't help to be condescending in return. Victoria Medvec (professor at the Kellogg School of Management, Northwestern University, cofounder and executive director of Kellogg Center for Executive Women, and CEO of Medvec & Associates) says that if it happens just once, you might want to simply ignore it.

"But if it's a common situation with the person, I would definitely address it," she says. "I will often refer to the comment I made earlier and say something like, 'As I said before, I definitely agree with this assessment or this point.' If you have a female colleague in the group, you can team up to address this as well and call out the offender for each other."

If the person is attempting to override you with incorrect information, you probably have to come on stronger. "Use a rich vocal tone, employing your abdominal muscles by bearing down on them when you're speaking," says Dr. Glass. "This will help show that you have gravitas. Then politely let him know that while you appreciate his input, he is mistaken and then explain why."

If it's a relative stranger doing the mansplaining, let's say a guy you're on an industry panel with, consider calling a spade a spade. Wall Street's Alexandra Lebenthal says that in a case like this, she believes it's perfectly fine to just call it out without seeming indignant. "Do it with some level of bemused shock. So, for example say, 'Oh my God, I think I just got mansplained!' Pretty simple but it works!"

A Gutsy Girl's Guide to Body Language

Our body language also plays a huge role in how others perceive us. It's easy to lose sight of your nonverbal cues when you're in the middle of a conversation or presentation, but the person you're engaged with won't miss them and will make certain assumptions, some on a subconscious level. Your posture comes into play, and so does the way you use your hands, the amount of eye contact you engage in, the sincerity of your smile (a sincere smile, sometimes referred to as a Duchenne smile, involves raising the corners of the mouth as well as raising the cheeks and producing crow's-feet), and so much more.

Your body language has the power to bolster your words but it can also undermine them. You may be telling a job interviewer that you have ten great years of experience that make you a perfect candidate for the position, but your lack of eye contact suggests you feel unsure.

There's so much to say about nonverbal communication (it's worth reading a book on it or articles online), but there are two main points a gutsy girl should keep in mind:

1. Exude *confidence*. This can be tricky when you're in tense

situations, such as a tough job interview or your first major presentation. Make a point to be conscious of your body language
and control it as much as possible. I remember prepping in my
thirties for an important speech, and when the speech coach
played back the video of my rehearsal, I was astonished to see
that I was literally wringing my hands during parts of the presentation. It was as if my body was shouting, "Oh, no, please tell
me I don't have to give this freaking speech."

It's possible, says Lillian Glass, to appear more confident
than you are in a given situation by adjusting your body language. Those tweaks, she adds, may even make you *feel* more
confident.

When it comes to projecting confidence, Glass believes there
are two factors to be particularly conscious of: keeping your
head up and your spine straight. "This kind of body language
indicates that you're powerful and not afraid, just as it does with
animals in the wild," she says. Follow this rule not only when
you're standing but also when you're sitting in a meeting or
interview. Sit up straight and don't slouch.

The amount of eye contact you engage in with someone is
also a key indicator of how comfortable you're feeling. When
you're listening to someone talk, hold his or her gaze. "You have
to be careful, though, especially in a job interview, that you
don't overdo it and make your eye contact too intense," Glass
says. She advises that you subtly rotate your gaze every couple
of seconds from the eyes of the speaker, to her nose, then her
mouth, then the entire face.

When you're in a situation in which you feel uncertain or
stressed, it's especially important to avoid "self soothers," like
playing with your hair or earring, licking your lips, touching

your neck, or rubbing your hands together. These immediately signal to others that you're nervous.

If you don't want to risk driving yourself nuts thinking about what every body part is saying, here's a very simple piece of wisdom from Glass: "Make it your goal to be *interested*, not interesting. Being focused on the other person and his or her message will make you feel less self-conscious and that will translate as confidence."

2. Exude *enthusiasm.* When I think of people who worked for me in the magazine business who later went on to do even bigger things, there's one clear point I recall about them. They walked into rooms as if they couldn't wait to be there, full of enthusiasm and energy. They wore their passion on their sleeves.

Bosses love and reward passion. It telegraphs that you're fully engaged in your work and want to succeed. Job interviewers love it, too. When asked about the biggest mistakes job candidates make, 55 percent of respondents in one study said lack of energy. Eliot Kaplan, former vice president of talent acquisition at Hearst, the company that owns magazines like *Harper's Bazaar* and *Cosmo*, told me that the most passionate, compelling job candidates tend to sit slightly *on the edge of their seats* during the interview. "It's lean in with a different meaning," he says. "Body posture during a job interview—or for that matter at any meeting—*matters*. Sitting up straight, leaning forward, seeming engaged says you're there, interested in what the interviewer is saying and how he or she is going to respond."

Think about that concept in terms of yourself. Do you sit on the edge of your seat both figuratively and literally? How would a stranger who saw you in a meeting grade your level of enthusiasm?

> ### Pay Attention to the Five-Second Comments People Make to You
>
> Are you sure you know how you come across? Gain a clue by noting little comments people make, like "You look so tired." They may be cheap shots but could also signal important info about how you appear to others daily.

A Short Course in the Art of Persuasion

There will be plenty of times in your career when you will need to use words to persuade someone to do something—like seeing your side of an issue, for instance, or changing direction altogether. There are whole books written on the subject, but here's a brief course in tactics used by Taylor Swift. *Yes*, Taylor Swift. I don't usually turn to Taylor for career tips but I'm a big fan of her ability to persuade. A few years ago Apple decided to offer a three-month trial period of its new streaming music service without paying royalties to performers, musicians, and producers. Swift wrote a powerful open letter to Apple on Tumblr protesting this decision and within twenty-four hours Apple changed course. Granted, Taylor Swift has a level of clout most of us will never approach, but her tactics were excellent and worth emulating.

She showed respect for the other side. Swift didn't come out with guns blazing or disparage the company she was in stark disagreement with. She titled her statement "To Apple, Love Taylor" and pointed out: "Apple has been and will continue to be one of my best partners."

As much as you may dislike the other player's position in an argument, remain calm, rational, and respectful or you'll put them quickly on the defensive.

Also try to get inside their heads. "If you want to try to persuade someone, it's really essential to try to see the situation from *their* perspective," says executive coach and organizational psychologist Ben Dattner. "If you're in tech and they're not, you aren't going to be speaking their language. Do what you can to figure out their language and speak in it."

She didn't make it all about her. If your goal seems self-serving to your opponent, you're far less likely to accomplish your mission than if you appear to be talking about *mutual* goals—meaning the goals of your organization or a project you're both working on. Or perhaps something bigger than both of you.

Swift said it perfectly. "These are not the complaints of a spoiled, petulant child. These are the echoed sentiments of every artist, writer and producer in my social circles."

She offered a powerful analogy. Analogies, as long as they're not hostile or ridiculous sounding, can go a long way toward helping the other side better see your point of view.

"We don't ask you for free iPhones," Swift pointed out. "Please don't ask us to provide you with our music for no compensation."

She clearly spelled out what she was aiming for. "It's not too late to change this policy," she told Apple. Meaning, "I'm counting on you to fix this now."

Simply complaining about what you dislike won't make a dent. You need to make clear what results you desire.

Just one more point about persuasion. Swift wasn't open to any compromise, so she never hinted at that. But in many situations you have to be willing to give some—or you won't end up with anything. Congresswoman Kathleen Rice, a highly regarded former prosecutor from Long Island, told me that for her, both in her days as a prosecutor and now as a politician, *pragmatism* has been key. "I might wildly disagree with my counterpart on a million issues, but we're at the table to find one inch of common ground that will allow us to get something done together. If I lose sight of that, then the whole thing was just a waste of my time."

Determine the areas you can agree on, discuss those, and see if meeting in the middle could work for both of you.

How to Toot Your Own Horn

One of the hardest things for a good girl to do is toot her own horn. She knows it's the right thing to do, but it can feel clunky and awkward and even obnoxious. But you have to. Because, trust me, your boss isn't always aware of your accomplishments.

- **Start by giving yourself permission.** Really, it's okay. Guys promote themselves all the time.
- **Don't feel you have to always make it about "we."** Women have been encouraged to highlight their wins by being inclusive, with comments like, "Great news. We convinced them to settle for only $10,000." Sure, "we" works in certain instances, particularly if your team was very involved. But always using "we" can come across as super earnest, even confusing. Sometimes it's just fine to announce, "Great news. I convinced them to settle for $10,000."

- **Seize a moment.** Margaret Milkint, managing partner of the Jacobson Group, a leading insurance recruitment company, says that a great way to toot your own horn is let it happen organically. "For instance, I got an email once from my boss wishing me happy holidays, and it became the perfect chance to share something I wasn't sure he was aware of," she says. "I told him I was enjoying being home, having my kids there for a visit, and also recharging my batteries after three new search engagements. The point is I wove in an opportunity to share my accomplishments in a natural, human, yet powerful way!"

Get Off Your Darn Email and into the Room

This whole chapter is about walking the walk and talking the talk, but here's something funny. These days we don't always give people we're dealing with an opportunity to actually see us walk and talk. We constantly rely on emails and texts to communicate, or at best phone calls.

But if you really want to win hearts and minds, go face-to-face. Nothing beats it.

"You have to be willing to get in the room sometimes," says Jen Furmaniak, CEO of JB Talent. "So many people, particularly millennials, prefer to do things by email rather than having direct contact. I built my business with a lot of face-to-face time. There's something to be said for showing up in a fabulous pair of shoes and looking great and confident and professional. Ask to meet in person. Meet for drinks. This is how you build relationships. And it's especially important early in your career. Go to lunch with other assistants. They will be great contacts later in your career."

Key Gutsy Girl Takeaways

- Dress for the job you aspire to, not the one you have.
- Speak for the job you aspire to as well.
- Get to the point when you speak, rather than describing the background info up front, and avoid phrases like, "Maybe we should…" or "I kind of think…"
- Be fully aware of the messages your body language is sending.
- Exude confidence and enthusiasm.

CHAPTER 5

A Gutsy Girl Asks for What She Wants (Even If There's a "Good" Reason She Shouldn't)

When Sony Pictures Entertainment was hacked in 2014, the troves of emails that surfaced revealed a stunning gender pay gap between not only Sony employees but also onscreen talent. Major case in point: Jennifer Lawrence's compensation for the Oscar-nominated film *American Hustle* was less than that of any of her three male costars, even though she was the biggest star.

Following the revelation, Lawrence penned a terrific essay for *Lenny Letter* and shared her surprising reaction.

"When the Sony hack happened and I found out how much less I was being compensated compared to the lucky people with dicks, I didn't get mad at Sony. I got mad at myself as a negotiator because I gave up early."

I love how Lawrence took partial responsibility. Women are still frequently treated unfairly when it comes to compensation, but in some instances we may have our good girl instincts partly to blame. We don't ask for we want and when we do, we aren't ambitious enough in our requests.

Why not? Perhaps in certain instances, you've been fearful of the possible consequences. You worried that if you pressed too hard during a salary discussion, it might have made the situation uncomfortable or even turned the other person against you. Lawrence admitted there was an element of wanting to be liked that influenced her decision to "close the deal without a fight." She didn't want to seem difficult or spoiled. She says that since that time, she's over trying to find the "adorable" way to make her case and still be likeable.

Like Lawrence, you need to squash your fear of rocking the boat and be willing to ask for what you want. You have to ask even at times when you think you shouldn't, ask boldly (without worrying you won't be "likeable"), and not give up if you initially meet with resistance.

The only answer when you don't ask is NO.

Why You Must *Always* Ask for the Money You Want

When I was in my late thirties, I was hired to be the editor in chief of a business magazine for women called *Working Woman*. The owner of the company promised me a nice salary bump and equity in the company. I was seven months pregnant when I took the job and crazy busy, and I showed up for work without seeing what the actual equity arrangement was. Dumb, I know. Five months into the job, after some pestering on my part, the company lawyer finally sent over the papers. I showed them to my accountant, Bob.

Bob was *not* happy with what he saw. He told me the plan was way too vague and that I should have discussed the arrangement when it was first mentioned. I admitted my mistake and asked if he could help me fix it. Bob told me that I needed to meet with the owner and ask for an equity arrangement that was much more defined. Sure, I could do that.

But that's not enough, Bob said. You've got to ask for a one-time payment to compensate for the months you haven't had equity. He suggested I ask for $50,000 in cash.

My jaw dropped. Bob, I told him, I work in the women's magazine field, not the Mafia. But Bob said if I didn't take action, I was a chump.

Well, I was just annoyed enough at myself to do it. I arranged to meet with the owner, put on my best power suit that day (we wore those back then), and told him I needed a clearer equity plan. He nodded, admitted I was right, and promised to provide one.

Now came the tricky part. I summoned my nerve, took a deep breath, and told the owner, "I need you to make up for the months I haven't had equity. I think $50,000 in cash would cover it."

Well, I was positive he was going to blow me out of the office. But *instead* he looked at me as if I were the savviest business-woman he'd ever met!

He said, "Okay, Kate, absolutely."

Well, I was thrilled that the ask paid off for me, though later I couldn't help but wonder, "Why didn't I ask for *$75,000?*"

I like to call that experience my "$50,000 moment of truth." It was the moment I learned that the squeaky wheel really *does* get the grease.

If you want a kickass salary, you can't count on the other side to just hand it to you. You're going to have to ask for it.

When *Why Good Girls Don't Get Ahead . . . but Gutsy Girls Do* was first published and I gave speeches on the nine principles, I could almost see the lightbulbs go on for women when

I addressed the importance of asking for the money they wanted. It was as if I was illuminating a thought that had just begun to gel in their brains. It's different nowadays. Women *know* how important it is to ask; they've heard that advice again and again. I'm sure I'm not telling you something you're unaware of.

But then explain this to me: If we know how important asking and negotiating are, why, according to a Glassdoor survey, did 68 percent of the women polled accept the first salary they were offered for their current positions? Are you part of that 68 percent?

Here's what I think is going on. Because asking for money makes us so uncomfortable, we end up talking ourselves *out* of it. If you're being offered a new job, for instance, you may think, "I'd better not ask because it'll make me seem difficult and I don't want to start on the wrong foot," or "What they're offering is in my range, so why not leave well enough alone?" or even "If I push too hard, they may rescind the offer." If you're due for a raise, you may tell yourself that your manager knows how strong your performance is and so you shouldn't even have to request an increase.

But you can't talk yourself out of asking for money, whether it's a starting salary, raise, or bonus, because if you do, you probably won't end up with what you deserve. Bosses *don't* always know what you want, or they may need to be reminded of the fact that you are indeed ready, or they may simply be looking for an excuse to save money in the budget.

And remember that even a little bump can make a big difference long term. According to a study by Michelle Marks and Crystal Harold of the George Mason School of Business, a twenty-five-year-old employee who negotiates a salary of $55,000 over the $50,000 that was offered will earn a whopping **$634,198** more in her lifetime by the time she reaches age sixty-five (assuming a 5 percent pay increase each year over a forty-year career).

The Gutsy Girl Asking Formula

Okay, I'm going to show you a very straightforward strategy for asking for the money you deserve. But first it's key to understand the basic principles behind it. Michelle Marks, now vice president for academic innovation and new ventures at George Mason University, says there are three key prerequisites for achieving your money goals, prerequisites she believes women often neglect:

1. Preparing in advance.
2. Negotiating the right way.
3. Understanding the importance of *total* compensation.

You must also use a salary discussion to be sure you understand everything about the role you are being offered. "You should never be negotiating only your salary," points out the Kellogg School's Victoria Medvec. "You should have a discussion about your employment, your role, responsibilities, initiatives important to the company that you are addressing, corporate goals, how success will be measured, timeline, title, and salary."

I know more than a few women who happily started their new jobs only to discover that they hadn't been given the title and/or authority they were expecting. If you're at a certain level, you'll need to determine whether or not you'll have an assistant (and if so, if that person will be shared), what resources you will have access to, what the spending budget will be (as well as your personal T&E), what type of workstation or office you will have, how many people will be reporting directly to you, and how many people you will be allowed to hire from the outside. Make sure everything is spelled out.

How to Negotiate a Great Starting Salary

Before you even walk through the door for the first interview, take a close look at your personal financial situation. If you're right out of college, figure out what salary you'll need to live on. If you're already working, it still pays to review your budget and perhaps think about your dream salary. What would you *like* to be making right now, considering, of course, your field, experience, and skill level.

If you're in your twenties, keep in mind that though your earning power will increase over time, what you make now becomes the platform on which future salary will be based.

After you've perused your finances, determine these two factors: (1) the *lowest* salary you are willing to accept based on your needs and desires; in negotiations this is called your reservation point. (2) Your BATNA, or "best alternative to a negotiated agreement." If you don't like the final number you are offered, what are your options? Are you being considered for other positions? Would you be content staying in your current job for a while? Based on your BATNA, you might want to review your reservation number.

Next, gather as much intel as you can about the going rate for the position in the marketplace (as well as perks and opportunities that come with it). Websites like Glassdoor .com, LinkedIn.com, PayScale.com, and Salary.com will offer clues, but not always the best ones. Reflect on the salary buzz you've heard as former colleagues have moved elsewhere. Read profiles of people in your field and see what hints are dropped. Ask your mentors if they have any insight on what the range might be for this job.

Now zero in and try to find out the range for the specific job you're being considered for. If you have a friend or trusted LinkedIn contact who is currently working in the company, or who used to work there, ask for input. That person may not be willing to do surveillance work on your behalf or, if close to the action, want to answer specifically, but he or she may be willing to give you a clue if you ask a slightly broad question like, "What do you think the salary *range* is for someone in this position?" Try to get a handle on what *men* in similar positions make as well as women.

Of course, if you've already had a preliminary interview, there's a chance you were told a salary range for the job (and you ideally didn't agree at that point to any amount).

Hopefully your intel provides you with a possible salary range, and that means you have a sense of the *other* side's reservation point, the highest amount they are prepared to offer you if you're the top candidate. It will also help if you gather any clues about *their* BATNA. Perhaps they have a very strong second candidate. Or the job is a new position and they could live without it for a while.

Using all the information you've gathered, determine what in negotiations is called the ZOPA, or the zone of possible agreement. That's the zone where your range overlaps with the range the employer is considering paying.

Let's say that from looking at your budget, factoring in your skills and the goals you have for yourself, and researching the field, you've determined that you'd be pretty happy with

$68,000 and thrilled with something in the low $70,000s (which seems possible for the field). You've also decided that you won't accept *less* than $60,000.

As for *their* range, you've determined that it's probably between $55,000 and $70,000.

If you lay the two ranges side by side, you will see that the ZOPA is between $60,000 and $70,000 (see diagram below). Which suggests you want to ask for $70,000.

But aim even *higher*. "In essence, your goal is to get as close as possible to their reservation point," says Medvec. "In order to achieve this, it is best to start beyond this point, as long as you can build a rationale for it." Aiming higher also protects you if your research has underestimated their range. So rather than asking for $70,000 at the start, boost it to $72,000 or even $74,000.

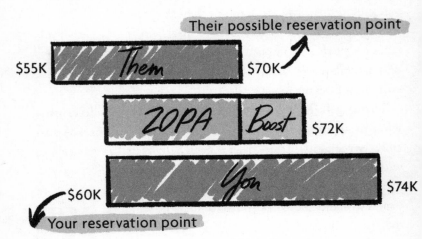

Zone of Possible Agreement (ZOPA)

Their possible reservation point

$55K **Them** $70K

ZOPA Boost $72K

$60K **You** $74K

Your reservation point

Okay, you've just been offered the job. If possible, be the one to open first with a number. The classic advice is to let the other side name the number, but some negotiation experts now say that it's actually in your best interest to go first.

"People do get a significant advantage from making the first offer in a negotiation," says Medvec. "When you go first, you create the starting point and get an anchoring advantage. In addition, when you lead, you are in the relationship enhancing position because you get to frame the negotiation, include the right issues, and be the one who looks flexible instead of going second and critiquing the other side's offer."

In more junior positions, however, that's not generally possible. "The offer of the job is confounded with the salary," Medvec points out. In other words, you are more likely to be told, "We would love to have you join our PR firm as an assistant. The salary is X amount."

Now prepare to negotiate. In a perfect world, the other side will offer you the exact salary you're hoping for or nod happily in agreement if you're the one who names the number. But the world isn't perfect and you'll probably have to do some negotiating (I would advise even negotiating if they name your dream number because the other side may be lowballing and willing to go even higher). As uncomfortable as this may be, try to see it as part of the process, something that's done all the time, and according to studies, more so by men than women. The first person who ever negotiated a salary with me was a guy (who I'd offered a senior editorship to) and he actually seemed to *relish* the process.

Okay, so let's say the other side went first and offered $66,000. Don't ask, "Is the salary negotiable?" because that gives them an out. Instead say something along the lines of, "I'd love to come to work here. The position sounds fantastic. But based on my experience and all I would like to contribute here, I was hoping for a salary of $72,000." Dr. Medvec highly recommends that you keep the focus as much as possible on the employer's needs/goals, and not your personal needs regarding money or your career plans for yourself.

Then be quiet. Don't rush to fill the vacuum. Give the other person the opportunity to counteroffer.

If he or she comes back with, let's say $68,000, there's no reason to give up yet because that may not be their reservation point. You could say something like, "Would you be willing to meet near the middle at $70,000?"

And what if *you* went first, asking for $72,000 and the other side counteroffered with only $68,000? Emphasize how excited you are about what you can contribute and that you hope they would be willing to go higher. Medvec recommends that in some situations, it's smart to offer a few options that look different to the potential employer. "One option," she says, "is a bet on your performance—with a bonus tied to performance metrics—so that you can demonstrate how confident you are that you can achieve the company's goals."

If you're still far from the number you'd like, this is the time to explore whether there are other ways to sweeten the deal. Would you settle for the offered amount if it came with three weeks vacation or the chance to work from home on Fridays? (See Thirty-One Perks to Consider Asking For, page 93.)

Don't panic if you're told, "I'll have to get back to you." Part of smart negotiating is being calm enough to wait. Just be sure to leave the other side with the impression that you really want the job and are excited about the possibility of working there. That way they won't be tempted to revert to their BATNA rather than produce a counteroffer.

Won't I Annoy People by Pressing for More?

"People doing the hiring often *expect* you to negotiate," says Michelle Marks, "and when you don't, you're leaving money on the table."

Granted, there may be some people who end up annoyed. According to a study done by Sheryl Sandberg's organization Lean In and McKinsey & Company, women who negotiate are more likely to be called bossy. But the bottom line is that if you come to an agreement, accept the job, and perform brilliantly, they're not going to care. I sometimes found myself mildly irritated by people who negotiated a far bigger salary than I'd planned to offer. But that was soon forgotten when they delivered fabulous results.

Thirty-One Perks to Consider Asking For

Here's a list of fairly common professional perks—benefits that many companies provide but in some cases only if you are gutsy enough to ask or negotiate for them. They're roughly in ascending order, starting with those that might accompany more junior positions, but these kinds of benefits often depend on the job and the field. For instance, if you go to work for a start-up, you could be entitled to equity even though it's your first job.

These are perks that can be used to sweeten a deal, but many might come with the job regardless. You just have to ask.

- Continuing education benefits/tuition reimbursement.
- Access to a mentoring program.
- Access to training seminars.
- Freedom to work at home.

- Flexible work hours.
- Revised timing of first raise (if your start date means you won't be reviewed for over twelve months).
- A guaranteed increase.
- A health/wellness stipend (i.e., gym membership, yoga classes).
- Marketplace discounts (this one is often automatic).
- A signing or re-signing bonus (this is common for senior-level execs but can happen farther down the ladder).
- Extra PTO (paid time off). Often easy for an employer to grant. Never neglect to ask about this.
- Relocation reimbursement.
- Equity or stock options (as I said, these are sometimes offered in entry-level jobs if the company is a start-up).
- A performance bonus.
- A *guaranteed* performance bonus.
- A phone, tablet, and/or laptop and service plan.
- Conference attendance.
- Home office furniture and supplies (particularly if you telecommute).
- Professional society dues.
- Club memberships.
- Reserved parking space.
- Business-class or first-class travel.
- A car.
- A car service.
- Financial/tax counseling.
- VIP service when traveling.
- An executive long-term incentive plan.
- Equity.
- Deferment of salary into a special high-interest account.

- A supplemental executive retirement plan (additional retirement compensation beyond what regular employees receive, sometimes including credit for more years than actually worked).
- A guaranteed severance package.

Keep in mind that there may be specific perks related to your field. If you teach at a university, for instance, you may be able to negotiate a special stipend for the summer months.

What if They Ask Your Current Salary?

Say, "I can understand your interest but my current salary doesn't actually reflect my experience or skills and what I could bring to this position. I'd like to focus on that." In some cities, it's even illegal for an employer to ask your salary history.

How to Negotiate a Great Raise (or Bonus)

This is a bit different than negotiating your starting salary. Be aware that your boss is probably working with a fixed pool of money, based on the economy and how well the company is doing, that must be distributed among everyone in the department.

- **Do plenty of homework.** Glean as much as you can about what people (especially men) in similar roles in the company are making, and listen for buzz about what new hires on or near your level are earning. Does your company have pay grades with minimum and maximum levels? If so, be sure you are familiar with them. Also learn as much as you can about the field you're in to gain a sense of what salary ranges are. Stay in the loop, too, about how your company is doing financially (read trade publications, pay attention to gossip). Most of all, engage in tough self-evaluation. Have you delivered a stellar performance during the past year? Then determine the ZOPA and the boost you should go for.

- **Be smart about timing.** Raises are often determined long before they are awarded, so have your raise discussion with your boss at least several months in advance.

- **Ask for a meeting.** Don't grab your boss in the hallway. Don't announce you want to talk about a raise. Simply email her, saying you'd like to get on her calendar.

- **Go first here with a number, too.** Be ambitious, knowing that your boss will mostly likely try to negotiate downward.

- **Make your case using concrete examples of the value you've brought.** Show measurable results, such as how much you've helped increase profitability or cut costs. There's nothing wrong with having some of it on paper.

- **Emphasize their needs, not just your own.** The focus should be about what you're going to do for your boss and the department. Besides discussing your performance, share some of your ideas for *next* year. Give your boss a sense of what you're going to be bringing to the table.

- **If your boss says her hands are tied, ask if she would be willing to mull it over and see if anything can be done.** When a boss's hands really *are* tied because the raise pool is limited, she might be willing to go "upstairs" and try to negotiate for more if her goal is to keep you happy.

- **If you've been turned down for the raise you want, do your best to learn why.** Is there a budget issue, for instance? Or is there a performance issue?
- **If a lower-than-hoped-for raise is related to budget, try to walk away with something else.** Check out the perks listed on page 93. Other items to consider asking for include a title change, a bonus (sometimes easier to give), a promise of another review in six months, or even a reclassification of your position.
- **Also ask for company perks that you didn't know to request when you started,** like a desk by the window or half an assistant.
- **If you've found out you're underpaid compared to others on your level, keep your voice neutral when discussing.** Say that you're aware of the discrepancy and that you'd like to find a solution as soon as possible. In certain cases this may be because you've been at the job for a while and raises often don't keep up with new starting salaries, which may be set by what's happening in the field.
- **Get a job offer from someplace else.** Some companies only give out bigger than average raises if you receive a firm offer from another company.

If You Suspect You're Underpaid, You Probably Are

That gut feeling you have that your salary sucks compared to others in your department? It's probably based on buzz you've been hearing about the industry and offhand comments from colleagues, and thus could very well be accurate. Let it be a kick in the butt.

Four Things You Absolutely Need to Ask for Besides Money

There's been a lot of talk lately about the importance of asking for more money, but don't lose sight of other things that are essential to ask for:

1. **Promotions.** According to a Lean In/McKinsey study, promotion rates for women lag behind those of men, and the disparity is largest at the first step up to manager—for every 100 women promoted, 130 men are. How to keep the numbers on your side? First, realize that you often have to *ask* for the promotion.

   I sometimes see women making the mistake of thinking they need to be tapped for that next big job. It doesn't always work that way. The best promotions you ever receive may be ones you initiate yourself. Set up a meeting with your boss and make your case with strong, well-prepared backup material.

   And second, focus on the job and not yourself. Don't make it about how much you deserve the position. When I was in the magazine business, it wasn't uncommon for me to see good girls finally summon the nerve to ask for a promotion only to have them make it all about themselves. They'd paid their dues, they'd say, or deserved it, or their husband had just taken a pay cut. I remember one note from someone who said, "I'm ready for the next step in my career." What your boss is ready for is what you can do for him. Spell out how much you have to contribute and the initiatives you'd love to launch. Even better, share tantaliz- ideas that you would like to execute in the new role.

2. **Opportunities.** Again, these don't always just get handed out. You have to ask for special projects and assignments, ones that will aid your boss, make her look good, ideally strengthen your strengths, force you out of your comfort zone, increase your confidence, enhance your reputation in the company, and ready you for promotions. And if no opportunity immediately presents itself, *create* one.

Ask, "What's missing here?" or "What problem can I help to solve for my boss or my department?" As a top executive I know points out, if you can't find something wrong, you're not looking hard enough.

But I'll say it again: Focus on the other side's needs, what you can do for your boss, the department, and your organization.

3. **Feedback.** Ideally your boss will give you feedback on your performance and assignments, but that doesn't always happen. If you aren't given feedback on an assignment or project, you should ask for it.

If it turns out your boss isn't happy with the way you executed a project, it's essential to figure out how you went astray. Some managers find it awkward when asked for a critique, so make it easier for your boss by making the discussion feel positive. Say, "I want to nail this next time. Can you tell me what would make it a hundred percent in your eyes?"

Though it's trickier to pull off, it can also be really beneficial to gather feedback on why you weren't offered a job you interviewed for. Wait a few days until after you've been turned down and then call the person doing the hiring. Don't try by email because the person won't want a record of the exchange. Say, "Would you mind me asking you for a bit of feedback? The job sounded really appealing and I would have loved to join the company. If I'm up for a similar position in the future, is there anything I can do to improve my chances?" The person may not be fully forthcoming with you, but you may come away with at least a hint you can use to your advantage.

4. **The job!** Oh, this one can feel nervy the first time you do it, but trust me, it pays off. At the end of a job interview, *ask for the business* (that's a term people in sales use). Say, "The job sounds even better than I imagined. I'd love the chance to show you what I can do."

Five Questions Every Intern Should Ask

1. "Can you evaluate my time here so I can learn even more from my experience?" (And if the evaluation isn't exactly what you were hoping for, show you are willing to take it to heart, as in, "Thank you so much. I will definitely consider what you said and use it to improve in the future." I worked with more than a few interns who didn't seem interested in gaining insight.

2. "I'm more convinced than ever that I'd love to work here once I graduate. What steps would you suggest I take between now and graduation?"

3. "When is the ideal time during my senior year to apply for a full-time position here?" It can vary tremendously depending on the field.

4. "I'm such a big admirer of yours. Would you mind if I stayed in touch?"

5. "May I use you as a reference?" (Never do this without permission.)

In Praise of Being Pushy, Grabby, and Persistent

When you want something, you often have to open your mouth and ask for it. But there are other things that are simply there for the taking—like a certain chair at a meeting or the chance to speak to a major player at a networking event. Rather than ask, you simply have to be brave enough to grab.

The first time I learned about the power of grabbing was when I won *Glamour* magazine's "Top Ten College Women" contest. Part of the prize was having our photographs taken for the August issue of the magazine. All the winners would appear in fashion spreads, and one lucky girl would be chosen for the cover. I wanted to be that girl.

During our prize trip to New York City, the other winners and I were shown to a giant fashion room with racks of clothes and told to pick out an outfit to be photographed in. Most of the clothes were in the muted earth tones that the fashion director explained were popular that year, but at the end of one rack I spotted a bright yellow turtleneck sweater with orange and green trim and a matching skirt. As the other girls rushed toward the heather and sage green separates, I made a beeline for the yellow sweater and grabbed it. I'd seen enough magazine covers to know that they had to pop, and I knew that yellow would pop like crazy.

I became *Glamour*'s August cover girl that year. Smiling like the cat that ate the canary in a bright yellow sweater.

I'd never advocate taking what clearly belongs to someone else. My point is simply to grab opportunities when they appear. And if they don't appear, produce them.

"When I first moved to LA," says screenwriter Sarah Heyward, "I noticed that among my friends who were trying to be actors, the most successful were the ones who were 'pushiest.' I took a real lesson from that when it came to pursuing my writing career. I sought out writers I admired, followed up with successful people I met at parties, and listened to advice from just about anyone who was willing to give it to me. Even now that I'm further along in my career, I'm still just as persistent. If there's a job I want, I will call and email whoever it takes until they either hire me or tell me to leave them alone."

So many men I've met are masters at grabbing what's there for the taking—and they never, ever feel apologetic about it. Be brave and borrow a page from them.

Key Gutsy Girl Takeaways

- Always ask for the money you want, no matter what reason there seems to be for not doing so.
- Don't worry that the other person will be annoyed. If you don't ask, you may actually be leaving money on the table.
- If the answer is no, keep negotiating. Walk away with *something*.
- Don't just ask for money. Ask for promotions and opportunities.
- Sometimes it's not about asking, but taking what's there to be taken. Grab and go.

CHAPTER 6

A Gutsy Girl Takes Smart Risks

In Chapter 1, I talked about the importance of generating big, bold, possibly disruptive ideas for your company, whether that company is one you work for, run, or own yourself. Generating ideas isn't enough, of course. You'll need to execute them. To do that you'll have to take risks, and in some cases that means putting your butt on the line.

Risk-taking is scary, I know. That's why good girls generally prefer to steer clear of it. But if you want to achieve dazzling results in your job and your career, you need to become a risk taker.

And that also means becoming comfortable with failing, because that's what risks sometimes lead to. Failure may sting and stress you out, but it's a way to learn, grow, gather critical info, and protect yourself against future failure. Executive coach Deb Busser, president of Energy Spring Leadership, says women need to give themselves permission to fail and be less than perfect.

"Women can work so hard at not being in a position to fail that we end up without any internal resources for dealing with it when we do," says Busser. "We need to recondition ourselves. When we sense that fear of failure or looking bad is coming into our decision making, we need to go all-in anyway."

Giving herself permission to fail made a huge difference for

Jen Glantz. About nine months after she started Bridesmaid forHire.com, she signed on with a service that pairs entrepreneurs with mentors. She ended up with an eighty-six-year-old man who had once been president of his own business.

"He didn't even know what a bridesmaid *was*," Glantz says, laughing, "but his advice has been wonderful. He told me I was being held back by my fear of failure. It was paralyzing me. Regrets, he said, make you human, but failure makes you a hero. Every week I have to present him with my list of failures for the week. He's made me see that the pain of failure isn't really so bad."

At the offices of theSkimm, the cheeky newsletter for people who want small bites of the day's happenings, taking chances—and even failing at those chances—is celebrated. Each week starts with a team meeting, during which the cofounders spotlight different projects teams are working on, but they also allow one team member to share a "failure" or a risk he or she took that didn't work out as planned. The point is to encourage the team to continue to experiment boldly.

How to Take Smart Risks (Because You Don't Want to Take Dumb Ones)

Though failure is always a possibility when you undertake a risk, you want to do your best to guard *against* it. Be as sure as possible the risk makes sense and has the potential to pay off brilliantly.

For me, risk-taking is always preceded by information gathering. You sometimes hear a business leader talk about relying mainly on his or her gut, but if you look closely, you'll discover that the person has been operating with a very *educated* gut, one born out of years of experience and data collecting. I felt during the years I worked in magazines that I had a really good gut, but it was definitely an educated one. I always did my research.

Before you take a risk, gather data. Study it without getting bogged down in it. Don't dismiss information simply because it runs against your thinking, though of course consider whether it might be biased.

It also really helps to develop **situational awareness**, or SA. It's a skill used by decision makers in aviation, the military, ship navigation, and emergency services. The Coast Guard defines *situational awareness* as "the ability to identify, process, and comprehend the critical elements of information about what is happening to the team with regards to the mission. More simply, it's *knowing what is going on around you.*"

Observe. Talk to people. *Listen.* Give yourself time to process what you hear and, again, don't dismiss a view being expressed simply because it's contrary to yours.

Ten Questions to Ask Before You Take a Risk

Once you've gathered your info, ask yourself the questions below. I put them together with Kristen Peed, director of corporate risk management at CBIZ, Inc., whose job is all about evaluating risks.

1. **What are the potential benefits of this risk?**

   _____

2. **What's the potential harm that could result?**

   _____

3. **How *probable* is the harm?**

   _____

4. **How severe could the harm be?**

_____

5. **How much can you afford to lose?**

_____

6. **Are you risking a lot for a little?**

_____

7. **What safeguards are in place to decrease the chance of harm?**

_____

8. **Can the risk be transferred or mitigated (perhaps by partnering with someone)?**

_____

9. **What is the risk of _not_ risking? (For instance, if you don't take this step, will a competitor do it, and will you then be missing out on a market opportunity?)**

_____

10. **Have you set up a way to monitor the risk?**

_____

Once you have your answers, consider them. Are the odds in your favor or not? Is the payoff worth it? Could you live with the loss? Be smart. Don't kid yourself.

Use this same tool with your career. For instance, how much would you risk by asking your boss to give you a new job title? Probably not a lot. But if you do an end run around him to present an idea to _his_ boss, that risk could be far more serious.

Risk-Taking Made Less Stressful

Even if a risk seems smart, it can still be stressful. Experiment and devise strategies that help you feel less anxious in these situations. That's something that's been essential for Julia Landauer, the Stanford-educated NASCAR driver and champion who started racing go-carts at age ten.

"Learning how to train your body and mind to deal with stress is so important," she says. "First, it's crucial to be able to recognize when you're stressed, scared, or nervous. Then, it's important to figure out how to treat those symptoms. Before races, I sprint to expel negative energy. Before high-stress meetings, I do the square method of breathing." (See The Square Method of Breathing, page 108.)

"And in any high-intensity situation," she adds, "I very narrowly focus on the steps that need to be taken in order to achieve the goal. While this comes somewhat naturally to me, I still need to remind myself to focus *solely* on the immediate task, not the big picture, consequences, or anything else."

When I wrote the original *Gutsy Girl* book, I had the chance to interview Frank Farley, the psychologist who formulated the concept of the Type T (thrill-seeking) personality. Farley found that some people are hardwired to find risk-taking appealing, and others, at the opposite end of the spectrum, are terrified of it. But if you're somewhere in the middle, you can become more comfortable with the process by simply practicing. "When you take a risk, it's very reinforcing," Farley told me. "There's a sense of exhilaration, empowerment, that feeling of 'I did it.'"

In other words, if you're a good girl who hasn't tried much risk-taking, put your toe in the water. Once you let yourself appreciate the rush, you're going to start thinking about getting your thighs wet, too.

The Square Method of Breathing

Square breathing, sometimes called *four-square breathing*, is a technique that reportedly relieves anxiety or panic and helps relax you. There are just four simple steps.

Inhale for 4 seconds.
Hold for 4 seconds.
Exhale for 4 seconds.
Hold for 4 seconds, then repeat the process.

How to Convince Others to Sign On for Risk

As you've heard me say before, some big ideas are best to launch without asking permission. If you're taking a smart risk and it's basically part of your job, there may be no reason you have to ask for approval. Just do it. But if you need your boss to sign off, do the following:

1. Speak passionately. Passion is contagious.
2. Concisely state your objective.
3. Spell out the why, stressing benefits.
4. Anticipate objections and present them as your own. For instance, say, "Now, of course, a major concern with this approach would be X, but as I investigated, I learned that this issue could be eliminated."

Fail Fast

When it starts to become apparent that a risk is going to backfire, assess, consider your options, and resist the urge to save something that probably can't be saved.

When I worked for the Hearst Corporation (running *Redbook* and later *Cosmopolitan*), I had the good fortune to be able to study the risk-taking strategies of two brilliant men, Frank Bennack Jr., the former CEO, and Gil Maurer, the former COO. Their approach just made so much sense. Gil summed up part of that strategy for me: "Fail *fast*. With smart risk, successes speak for themselves and receive follow-up investment. Disappointments are minimized in that they're quickly identified and suspended, and not allowed to become a drain on resources."

Letting go is often the smartest course of action.

How to Learn from a Dud

Though you don't want to agonize about your losses, or endlessly ruminate about a setback (more on worrying in Chapter 7), it really helps to summon all your gutsiness and study your mistakes, learning what you can from them. That will help reduce the risk of failure going forward.

When I was the editor in chief of *Cosmo*, newsstand sales were a significant contributor to the bottom line, and as those sales grew, my goal became to have 2 million newsstand buyers each month. My winning covers fortunately outnumbered the losing ones, but I definitely had some stinkers over the years.

It's never fun to stare a failure in the face, but I made myself do it. Whenever I had a dud, I'd conduct what I came to call "the rug test." I'd toss the issue down on the carpet in my office. Just above it, I'd lay a row of top-selling covers from previous months and below it I'd put past losers. Then I'd spend about an hour making comparisons. What did the current issue have in common with other failures? What *didn't* it have in common with the winners? At times I felt like someone on a CSI team, examining a corpse at a crime scene and trying to determine the exact cause of death.

And guess what? By the time I was done studying all those issues, I'd gained insight. I could make a good guess as to why the cover hadn't worked, a factor (unfortunately) I'd been too close to to determine previously. Maybe the outfit on the actress or model was all wrong—or at least wrong for the season. Or maybe the cover lines were too vague and just not compelling enough. Looking backward enabled me to be smarter about how I moved forward.

When a risk bombs or even just falls flat:

- **Analyze whatever data you can put your hands on.** It also helps to pump people who might have something truly valuable to say (like your consumers or customers). And don't become defensive. Trendera CEO Jane Buckingham says one of the big mistakes she sees clients make is rationalizing unpleasant findings that research turns up.
- **Spell out what you're seeing.** One of the discoveries that emerged when I studied newsstand failures was that the size of the model's or actress's head seemed to affect sales. Turns out *Cosmo* readers didn't like pinheads!
- **Take action.** Now come up with your plan for the future. For instance, I actually ended up tracing the model and celebrity heads on a bunch of winning covers and created

a template for my design director to use so that she always made sure the photo we were using on a cover was blown up to the right size.

- **Accept responsibility, learn, and then let go.** I once worked with an executive who always blamed everyone except her own department for any setbacks that occurred in her area. It was always, *always* someone else's fault. Suck it up and take responsibility. If you don't acknowledge your mistakes, you look like a wimp and you lower your chances of learning from them.

Some risks don't just leave you with regrets; they make you absolutely cringe inside. No matter how painful, face up to them and internalize the lessons. Early in her career, Sally Susman, Pfizer's dynamic executive vice president of corporate affairs, worked for a senator on Capitol Hill. She knew that he was planning to announce his retirement after a long and successful career, but it would all be done on a specific timetable. "In a moment of youthful indiscretion," she says, "I told one friend...who told one friend...who told one friend. Before I knew it, word was out and the media was calling. I was the source of a leak that caused a respected leader to have to react on defense. My apology did not lessen the shame I felt for a long time. It was a great lesson about how sacred trust is. I have never since broken a trust, and consider myself a citadel of confidentiality—an essential quality in my role as head of corporate affairs and communications."

Why You Should Analyze Your Wins, Too

When a risk pays off, it's easy to pat yourself on the back and begin iterating. But you want to grasp as best you can why the risk paid off. There's even a chance it wasn't for the exact reasons you assumed. Some factor you weren't fully aware of may have played a role.

Fairly early in Keira Knightley's acting career, I ran a cover of her that ended up being a huge seller. She looked beautiful, with her dark hair super glossy and full. She was dressed in jeans and a tight, striking pink and black top by Chloé, and we made the background hot pink to match the top. After the blockbuster numbers came in, I, of course, was panting to run another Keira Knightly cover as soon as possible.

But when we conducted a series of focus groups a few months later, asking readers to talk about covers they loved, I was shocked to discover that most of the women in the groups who had purchased that issue didn't even know who Keira was. She wasn't a major star yet. They'd made the purchase, they said, because of how luscious the whole package was.

What I really needed, I realized, wasn't necessarily another Keira cover, but one that featured that same shade of pink and maybe another killer Chloé top.

Analyzing your wins will help you craft a winning formula.

But remember, no formula lasts forever, or even for long. That's why you need to be taking new risks all the time, testing new ideas and new directions. Which leads me to my next point!

Be a Risk Agent

We hear a lot these days about the importance of being a change agent, someone who stimulates and facilitates change rather than just waiting around for it to happen. I think it's also important to think of yourself as a *risk* agent, a gutsy girl who constantly keeps her eyes open for opportunities to change things up in a really big, possibly disruptive, way, even if it involves serious risk *and*—here's something you don't hear as much about—even when there doesn't appear to be a pressing need for disruption.

When Ursula Burns, former president of Xerox, was interviewed by the *New York Times*, she made a comment that I liked so much, I jotted it down. She told the reporter that she keenly admired people in her company who *actively* took risks, who were always on the lookout for ways to destabilize. "Fix it," she said, "well before you have to."

Such sage advice.

One of the smartest risks I ever took was one that didn't, at least at the time, seem necessary. It was a few years into my tenure at *Cosmo* and newsstand sales were terrific. But just as I believe that the time to look for a new job is when you're happiest at your current one, I think the time to consider risk and change in your business is when things are going fabulously.

For me, it started with a bit of situational awareness. I'd begun to note that whenever one of my senior editors or I interviewed female job candidates, they often mentioned the men's magazine *Maxim* as one of their favorite publications. At first that seemed kind of odd. But as I thought about it, I realized these Gen X (and later Gen Y) women loved the cheeky, irreverent humor of *Maxim*. The *Cosmo* I'd inherited was fun and over the top, but hardly cheeky. What I began to understand was that young women now craved that kind of humor in a magazine. I decided to make a series of changes in *Cosmo*. I added a totally irreverent tone to many of the stories and introduced several humor columns, including one by two men. The sales spike was almost immediate. And fortunately rumors that *Maxim* was considering introducing a magazine for women subsided. I like to think I closed a hole in the marketplace.

I'd taken a risk and fixed a problem before it was broken. And it paid off perfectly. So:

- Note systems and processes that have been there for ages and ask how you might shake them up.
- Stay on top of trends in the marketplace and consider how they could play into your department or company's vision.
- Pay attention to what makes you nervous (like what a competitor is up to). Instead of running from it, let it inspire you to take a risk that will pay off big-time.

In Fact, Take a Risk Every Day

Because *Cosmo*'s identity as a magazine was about being fun, fearless, totally candid, and often over the top, I established the habit of asking myself each morning, "What am I going to do to break the law today?"

I actually think it's smart to ask yourself a variation of that on a daily basis no matter what field you're in: "What risk am I going to take before the day is over?" Don't settle into a comfort zone in which you fail to be an active risk taker.

Question the way something's always been done, look at situations from a totally fresh angle, consider a totally far-fetched idea, and approach projects using the four B's I mentioned in Chapter 1.

Bear in mind that regular small risk-taking can pay off, too. Recently I had the opportunity to hear a talk with Gretchen

Carlson, the former Fox News commentator who was brave enough to sue the network for sexual harassment. She mentioned some of the little risks she took early in her career to help her develop as a reporter—for instance, deciding to walk as she did a live shot instead of just standing in one place. "Take risks instead of being perfect," she challenged the audience.

Dumb Risks Generally Not Worth Taking

- Going around your boss to pitch an idea to someone higher up
- Trying to hide bad news from your boss
- Sending an email that explains how freaking annoyed you are with someone
- Dating a coworker when it's against policy
- Dating your boss
- Dating a subordinate
- Working your side hustle at the expense of your job
- Bad-mouthing your boss during an exit interview

The Glass Cliff Risk

That's right, not glass *ceiling*, but glass cliff. In 2004 two professors from the University of Exeter in England, Michelle Ryan and Alex Haslam, coined the term *glass cliff* to describe a phenomenon they saw emerging: that women are more likely to be appointed to leadership roles, such as executives in the corporate world, academics, and political election candidates, during times of crisis, which meant the chances of failure are greater. Later studies of Fortune 500 companies backed up their findings.

So, should you grab a wonderful but high-risk career opportunity? Could it be a glass cliff? Executive coach Deb Busser suggests evaluating first by asking yourself these questions:

- What are the potential upsides as well as the potential downsides of the job?
- What is my level of social capital inside the organization? Do I have a few trusted colleagues who will get on board? What about outside? Do I have people from the outside who would want to join or at least be used as an informal board of directors?
- How ready is the organization for change? Is it a glass cliff because the organization can't tolerate the status quo anymore? With a greater level of riskiness, there may also be a greater level of readiness for change.
- Does it sound like fun?
- What will I learn that I couldn't by not taking the role? Will it up-level my brand and negotiating power for future positions?
- If it is widely perceived to be a tough slog, what intangible can I negotiate around work hours, time off, and so on?
- Can I negotiate some variable comp for certain milestones?
- Can I get extra consideration in a severance package if things don't work out?

I know risk-taking is scary. The first time I was booked to be on the *Today Show*, I briefly toyed with the idea of pretending to pass out in the green room so I wouldn't have to do it. But as Frank Farley pointed out, the rewards that risk-taking brings will make it easier over time. Every good thing that happened in my career came from taking a risk.

So tell yourself you'll take one first thing tomorrow. And then every day going forward.

Key Gutsy Girl Takeaways

- Take *smart* risks. Determine not only possible benefits but also the downsides.
- Study your duds. What can you learn from them? Study your wins, too. Make sure you know the real reason why they worked.
- Fail fast. Don't stick with something that isn't working.
- Be a risk agent. Don't simply respond to opportunities presented. *Look* for risks.

CHAPTER 7

A Gutsy Girl Doesn't Need All the Likes

As I mentioned earlier, when I was in my late thirties and working as the editor in chief of a parenting magazine (and also seven months pregnant with my second child), I was invited to interview for the job of running *Working Woman*, a business magazine for women. I went to the meeting in a pair of maternity pants and to my shock was offered the position. I accepted. The idea of the magazine intrigued me, there would be a nice bump in salary, and since I would soon have two kids, I appreciated the idea of running a magazine with a bigger staff and far more resources than I currently had at my disposal.

The weekend before I started, I did a more thorough dive into the magazine and realized to my dismay that it seemed really foreign to me. The pages were filled with dense, dry articles on narrow, very specialized topics with headlines such as "How Leasing Employees Saves Time and Money," "Sweet Success in Sales Automation," and "How to Keep Your Finger on the Pulse of Productivity." The reader obviously spoke some kind of secret language, one I hadn't learned working at magazines like *Glamour* and *Child*.

Before long, I began to experience this sickening dread that

I had bitten off more than I could chew. How could I generate ideas on subject matter I knew nothing about? It was as if I'd accepted the job as editor in chief of *Astrophysics* magazine or, worse, had accepted a job *as* an astrophysicist. I was going to fail, I realized, and totally embarrass myself.

My husband, suspecting my distress, tried to comfort me. "It's just new-job anxiety," he said.

"No, it isn't," I snapped. "I can't do this job. I know nothing about the topics, nothing about the reader."

"How can you say that?" he asked, astonished. "Aren't *you* a working woman?"

I thought a moment and then began to laugh. He was right, of course. I might not have experience covering business, but I *was* a working woman, one who was currently the head of a magazine and was executing a winning strategy, supervising people, overseeing a budget, hiring and firing, and thus I shared a lot with the *Working Woman* reader. I wasn't nearly the outsider I'd convinced myself I was.

Once I took over the magazine, I found I loved providing women with advice on career and business subjects, though I made the features more universal (and, I like to think, compelling) than what had run previously. I had not only worried unnecessarily but had practically *catastrophized* the situation.

I think many women can relate to the dilemma I found myself in that weekend. When the going gets tough, we often agonize, project, decide that disaster is imminent, and anxiously anticipate people's disapproval.

"In some ways as women, we're hardwired to worry," says New York City psychologist and author Dale Atkins, PhD. "Our instinct is to protect, to take care of people. If we don't protect, something can go wrong. A certain amount of that is healthy. It's when you go overboard that problems can occur."

And it's not just ourselves we worry about. "Women seem to take into account so many data points when they're making any kind of decision," says the Female Quotient's Emma Smith-Stevens. "We worry not only about how a decision we make might change our own lives but how it will affect other people. If it's about a promotion, we may worry about the person who *won't* be getting the promotion. If it's about a raise, we may even worry that if we're given too high of an amount, there won't be enough money for the company group dinner that's being planned. Guys, on the other hand, seem to stay focused on the objective."

Things a Good Girl Worries about Way Too Much

- Getting it wrong
- How badly things will turn out if she *does* get it wrong
- What will happen to her personally if the worst happens
- Whether people really like her
- What something she notices *really* means

All that worrying doesn't simply produce headaches, heartburn, and stomach cramps. It may also slow you down and sometimes even paralyze you. It can influence your decision making, compelling you at times to pick the safe choice rather than the smart, risky one, or perhaps no choice at all. It can make you overeager to please, because you want to guard your flank.

And there's something else. Intense worrying can also negatively impact the impression people have of you as a leader or potential leader. According to Nancy Parsons, executive coach, president of CDR Assessment Group, and author of *Fresh*

Insights to End the Glass Ceiling, getting mired in worry can thwart a woman's attempt to reach the top tier in her company. Parsons's research of executives has shed light on what she calls the unrecognized reality that in challenging situations, women leaders often go in to "worrier mode," based on fear of failure and fear of making a mistake.

"When under conflict or adversity, women often resort to studying, analyzing, and re-studying," says Parsons. "This fearful, cautious, and moving-away-from-conflict approach results in them being judged as lacking in courage and confidence. There are unwritten expectations that leaders do not, and should not, run away or back down from the tough issues or conflict."

It would be inhuman not to worry at times, but gutsy girls know how to keep worry at bay as much as possible and not look undone by it.

How to Worry Less in Tough Situations

If you're a worrier at heart, you can't just stop because I told you to. "These traits stay with us," says Parsons. But over time, she points out, you can make key adjustments. "You can manage to neutralize your tendency to over worry and prevent it from interfering with your performance."

Start by following a piece of age-old advice. Ask: "What's the worst that can happen?" According to Dr. Atkins, that approach can really help. Unless, she says, you suffer from extreme anxiety, which could make thinking about the situation worse, it's instructive to play the scenario out in your head and consider the possible ramifications. More than likely, it won't be anything you couldn't handle.

Ask yourself the following:

- **What's the worst that could happen?**

  _____

- **What's the likelihood of the worst happening?**

  _____

- **What strengths would you bring to the situation if the worst happened?**

  _____

- **How have you coped in any similar worst-case scenarios in the past?**

  _____

- **What's your plan for handling the worst if it actually does happen?**

  _____

Going through this exercise allows you to see that even if the outcome is bad, you will have a way of dealing.

It can also be helpful to use a friend (not a work colleague) as a sounding board. A friend can remind you of your core strengths (like my husband saying I *was* a working woman) and how you've coped with challenging situations in the past.

What's key, says Parsons, is to try to catch yourself before going into worry mode because it's easier to neutralize the tendency to worry than to eliminate your tension and anxiety when you're in the thick of it. Note the worry beginning to build, ask yourself what triggered it, and refuse to allow your buttons to be pushed.

How to Stop Taking Things Personally (or the Little Trick You Can Steal from Dudes)

Though some worrying relates to what might happen in the future, other times good girls fret about what's just transpired. For instance, let's say you've walked out of a meeting that didn't go as well as you'd hoped or you presented an idea that generated what seemed like a lukewarm response from your boss, or maybe you had an encounter with a colleague who seemed uncharacteristically curt.

As soon as it's over, you may start to stew or ruminate. You may even torture yourself, asking questions, like, "What did that *mean*?" "Did I just blow that?" "Does my boss not like me anymore?" Stop rehashing.

"Some of the best advice I got in my career came from men at the Bureau, including my deputies," says Lauren Anderson, former FBI executive and geopolitical/international security consultant. "One of them told me I had to stop Monday morning quarterbacking myself after a meeting. Although I never said anything, he saw it and told me, 'Let it go, stop caring about it because none of the guys are. They walk out of the meeting and it's done.'"

Sure, in some cases, a comment or vibe might actually mean something, but not necessarily something about YOU.

"In my coaching, I sometimes see women take things personally when there's no reason to," says executive coach Deb Busser. "They assign a meaning that isn't there. For instance I worked recently with a female executive who'd just had an uncomfortable interaction with a very difficult man, and she was upset that she might have done something wrong. But since I'd been present, I could see that she hadn't done anything wrong. The guy simply had a problem with authority—hers or anyone else's."

Over the years I've found that men have a remarkable ability to look at possibly negative experiences and not take them personally, or they recast them in a positive light. They come up with their own special words to characterize a setback or awkward encounter, often making it neutral rather than negative, and impersonal rather than personal. For instance, a guy doesn't announce, "They hated my idea." He says, "They decided to go in another direction." Reframing can spare you a lot of angst.

That's not to say you should ignore warnings. I'm all for a healthy dose of paranoia at work. If your boss has been in a series of closed-door meetings and looks agitated during the day, trouble may be brewing, trouble involving her position or even the company, and you'll want to keep your ear to the ground.

In general, however, don't fret unless there's a decent reason to. If a moment gives you pause, ask yourself these key questions before jumping to any conclusion:

- **What other explanation could there be for what just happened besides the one you're worrying about?**

  _____

- **Does this new explanation line up with other information you have?**

  _____

- **Will anything bad happen if, for the time being, you accept this alternative explanation?**

  _____

- **Is there a way to gather more information without making yourself feel or look crazy?**

  _____

- **Are you using the rule of two? If so, what are you picking up?**

   This is a rule of mine that has proved extremely beneficial. If one thing gives you a weird feeling, let it go, but if something similar happens, take note and ask yourself, "What is the underlying message here?" Then take action. Midway through my magazine career, I had lunch with the president of the company, whom I reported to, and I noticed he seemed fairly distracted. Okay, that was odd for him, but I didn't let it bug me. A few weeks later when I called his office, his assistant said he was out of town and I realized that my boss seemed to be away A LOT lately, also unusual. Message: He didn't seem fully engaged anymore. Rather than just worrying about it, I made a point of spending more time with the number two. Several months later, my boss resigned to run another company. And the number two, whom I now had an even better rapport with, got the top job.

   _____

- **If you decide that something negative really is going on, how can you effectively respond?**

   _____

Okay, Let's Say You Really *Do* Have Something to Worry About

Your boss is definitely giving you the cold shoulder. Bosses can sometimes be bad at letting you know there's a performance issue. Instead, they act cool or sulky or exclude you from meetings and conversations. Take the bull by the horns. Don't ask,

"Is something the matter?" which could box him into a corner and possibly cast the situation in a more negative light than he actually views it in. Instead say, "I'd love to sit down and review my goals with you so I'm sure I'm hitting the targets you want me to hit." If there *is* an issue, this will allow him to express it. Then follow the advice in "The Gutsy Girl's Guide to Accepting Criticism" (see page 131).

You've made a big blunder. If there's no reason for your boss to know, don't volunteer the info. Just fix it. If your boss must know or is likely to find out, calmly spell out the problem, apologize if it's warranted, and present the *solution*, at the same time remaining as positive as possible. You could say something like, "I've got a good understanding of what went wrong and I'm doing X and Y to address it and make sure it doesn't happen again." Don't make excuses. Listen to feedback.

A colleague is making trouble for you (i.e., bad-mouthing you, poaching ideas, or muscling into your territory). The first time this happens, you may tell yourself to let it go rather than confront the person, which can be uncomfortable. But I've found that letting it go is equal to giving the person permission to do it again. You have to be gutsy and face it head-on. "When there's a conflict," says Sarah Friar, CFO of Square, "you need to explain what you're doing and why you're doing it."

Ask to speak to the person privately. Be firm, but not confrontational, stating the facts, says executive coach Ben Dattner, rather than drawing inference. "If a peer didn't CC you on an important memo," he says, "instead of asking, 'Why are you trying to keep me out of the loop?' try, 'I'm sure it was an over-sight, but I need to be included on these going forward.'"

Sometimes trouble comes in the form of a male peer who seems dismissive of you and your ideas. It's possible he has an underlying issue dealing with women. If you confront him, he may very well insist that you're imagining it. A better strategy may be to ask the offender for coffee or lunch and try to get to know him. Ask questions about his background, how he enjoys spending time. Let him begin to see you as a person and not someone who he needs to feel threatened by. From there, share information that he'll find useful. Support his ideas in meetings. Even suggest collaborating on a project.

And what if the peer who's creating the problem doesn't cease and desist? Should you get tough? That really depends on your company culture and the circumstances. But here's an old adage worth considering: *Never wrestle with a pig. You both get dirty and the pig likes it.* In other words, if things ratchet up, it could cause problems for *you.*

A better approach, says executive coach Liz Bentley, is to "stick with what you're doing and be patient. Bosses eventually spot those behaving badly."

Ben Dattner agrees. "Sunlight is the best disinfectant. Sooner or later, things come to light." But protect yourself as much as possible with a trail of visibility, like CCing the right people on a pertinent email that proves you *are* sticking to what's important.

If you're having a problem with a peer, do what you can to avoid having to go to your boss, because in my experience, most bosses don't like to have to referee these issues. If you finally decide the situation is serious enough to require your boss's input, don't sound like a tattletale. Explain the issue calmly and unemotionally, describe what you see as possible solutions, and ask your boss for input.

A male colleague is sexually harassing you. Maybe the first time he made a suggestive comment, you ignored it, thinking you might have misheard. But now he's said it again and you know you heard it right. Don't let it go again. Before approaching HR, see if you can shut things down yourself. Tell him in a firm voice that his comments make you uncomfortable and you want him to stop. Immediately, loop in your boss or a trusted coworker so that someone can corroborate the situation later if necessary. If he doesn't stop or retaliates somehow, go immediately to HR. Though many women have faced nightmarish sagas, good companies take sexual harassment seriously, especially now, and HR will investigate and ideally take action.

Your latest project has just derailed. Don't guess at the reason. Gather data quickly. Loop in those on your team whose input will be valuable, though do your best not to look rattled. Listen and ask for input. Determine as fast as possible the steps that must be taken and then pull the trigger. If the derailment is due to a subordinate's blunder, do a one-on-one debriefing, remaining as neutral as possible so the person reveals all that you need to know.

Everything is going to hell. Stop what you're doing, take some deep breaths, and assess. That's what San Francisco–based attorney Christina Tabacco learned when she trained to be a safari guide in South Africa, and it's great advice in any work situation. "The guides who knew the bush best had some incredible ability to let a harrowing moment stretch before them, absorbing what was unfolding," she says. "The waiting, while painful for those of us new to the bush, often caused the situation to disband or deescalate without 'doing' much at all."

Use this time to get a firm grasp of what the real issues are and create an action plan.

Don't Let Them See You Sweat

As stressed as you feel when something goes wrong, you have to do your best not to *show* it, especially to your boss and upper management. In fact, you may need to overcompensate.

In her assessment studies of executives, Parsons has found that men in executive positions are more likely to win the perception battle during any kind of adversity. "They stay in the game with stamina, pushing forward hard and fast, sometimes in an over-the-top, pushy way," she says. "They fight for resources, fight for airtime, and aggressively win the day. Women under pressure, however, tend to be cautious decision makers and slow up the process. They get quiet in meetings, run away, study, and analyze some more."

What Parsons found is that the behavior men typically display in adversity ended up being viewed as "leader-like" by promotional power brokers. Women who came across as being in "worrier mode" were not. They were viewed as fearful, indecisive, and lacking in courage.

No matter how much a situation scares you, don't retreat. Stay totally in the game.

The following diagram gives important steps that Parsons recommends.

How Not to Look Like a Hot Mess

When a high-ranking female TV executive ran into trouble a few years ago, a colleague anonymously deemed her "a hot mess" in a major magazine article.

You never, ever want anyone to view you that way. If you don't look in control, it will undermine the steps you are taking to *be* in control. Practice square breathing (see page 108). Don't overdo caffeine or skip exercise. Even if you're burning the midnight oil, don't forgo shampoos, blowouts, and makeup. Exuding calm can actually make you calmer.

The Gutsy Girl's Guide to Accepting Criticism

One of the things a good girl dreads is being criticized by her supervisor. That's never fun, of course, but valid criticism is an essential tool for developing your skills and judgment.

"I see women sometimes become super sensitive and defensive when criticized," says Busser. "They may refuse to take feedback or their resistance comes through in more subtle ways—like through their body language."

In the past, how have you responded when your boss spoke negatively about your performance? Did you pay close attention, take notes, and promise to work on the issue? Or did you become prickly, sullen, tearful, or argumentative? When you resist criticism, you shut down important communication with your boss not only in that moment, but also perhaps in the long term.

Some studies have suggested that bosses sometimes avoid giving criticism to women who take it too personally. But you don't want that to happen. You need to hear what the issues are so you can address them.

A non-perfect performance review allows you to "see your truth," says Liz Bentley. "It can be both enlightening and powerful."

The next time your boss criticizes you, take these gutsy steps. They will pay off big for you in the future:

- Listen. Really listen. Don't interrupt. Look engaged. And ask questions when it's appropriate. "This is a time to get *curious*," says Busser. "Ask for further explanation if you aren't clear. You can say something like, 'Would you mind giving me an example of X so I better understand?'" If it's criticism about something major, like an assignment, jotting down notes during the discussion can be helpful.

- Take a deep breath and detach. This is not about your self-worth. This is about obtaining valuable insight even if it stings or is delivered poorly.

- Now repeat back, as undefensively as you can possibly manage, the gist of what your boss said. This guarantees that you've processed the information correctly (which can be difficult when you're under stress), and can help the conversation go more smoothly.

- Then offer a solution. Ideally your boss will have suggestions, but you can't necessarily count on it. Let's say she criticizes you because she feels you don't keep her abreast enough of what you're working on. You can say something like, "What if I gave you a thorough update by email every Friday? Or would you prefer in person?"

- After the meeting ends, shoot your boss an email recapping what you discussed. No need to focus on the negatives. Instead, thank her for the feedback and spell out the positive steps you intend to take and when.

- Nip denial in the bud. Before you complain to a friend or your partner about the unfairness of it all, be gutsy enough to acknowledge how much of the criticism is warranted. If your performance really isn't up to par, try to understand why. For instance, "If your boss has complained that you aren't getting material in on time, ask yourself, 'Why *am* I procrastinating?'" says psychologist Atkins. "'What's going on here?'"

- If the criticism is part of a 360 critique (God, who invented those?), take time to process the information without letting it irk you. Random anonymous comments can probably be ignored, but don't overlook consistent negative comments. Is there truth there? Do you need to address it?

- What if the criticism isn't warranted? It's still essential to acknowledge the perception. ("I can see how you would have drawn this conclusion...") Then offer a game plan on correcting that perception.

What to Do if You Start to Cry

We know it's generally not smart to cry at work, even in front of a generally sympathetic boss or supportive peers. But sometimes, during a tough moment in a meeting or review, it just happens. If you can't get control of your tears, politely excuse yourself. Instead of saying, "I'm feeling too emotional," you could say, "I'm just very passionate on this subject." In a recent study, Harvard Business School doctoral student Elizabeth Baily Wolf and colleagues found that people saying they were "passionate" after displaying distress were viewed as more competent than if they admitted to being "emotional." Or simply say, "I need a few minutes. If you don't mind, I'd like to discuss later in the day."

If there's one thing I wish I'd known years ago that I know for sure today is that 99 percent of things I worried about never materialized into anything I couldn't fix.

Key Gutsy Girl Takeaways

- Worry less by asking yourself what's the worst that could happen.
- Confront trouble rather than wishing it will go away on its own.
- Don't let them see you sweat. If something goes wrong, engage, speak up, show you're in control. Don't back away.
- See criticism as a powerful tool for development. Listen. Accept. Learn.

CHAPTER 8

A Gutsy Girl Owns Her Excellence

The woman I was speaking to seemed liked a total dynamo and also incredibly well informed. We were strangers but had introduced ourselves to each other during the networking portion of an event. "What do you do professionally?" I asked a few minutes into the conversation. Her reply: "I consult with companies about upcoming trends."

It was only after we'd parted, when I looked at the business card she gave me, that I saw she was actually president of her own research company.

Women often downplay what they do, what their skills are, and their ambitions for the future. It's as if we're fearful of sounding too braggy and having that work against us.

You have to be gutsy enough to own your excellence and your ambition, to announce, "This is who I am, this is what I know how to do, and this is what I want for myself." Practice will make it a lot easier.

When you fail to own your excellence and ambition, the problem isn't simply that you sound overly modest while networking or during interviews. It affects your actions, too. It makes you apologetic, tentative, hesitant to speak up, and reluctant to step forward. And that can really screw up your trajectory.

Owning your excellence and ambition means:

- exuding confidence;
- not apologizing for who you are and what you want;
- looking, sounding, and acting the part;
- expressing your ideas and opinions effectively;
- feeling entitled to and requesting the access, information, and resources you need (and deserve);
- embracing your *readiness* for a new job, promotion, or opportunity;
- becoming the relentless architect of your career.

Little but Powerful Confidence-Building Tricks

During the Harvard Business School Women's Leadership Forum that I took part in, the sixty-plus participants ate lunch together every day and we used that opportunity to discuss a myriad of work topics. One day the subject of imposter syndrome came up and everyone at my table admitted experiencing it at times, including this fabulous, clearly kickass woman who ran a maximum-security prison!

It didn't surprise me. I often hear amazingly successful women describe moments when their hard-won confidence inexplicably vanishes in a critical situation. They talk about their "inner critic" taking over or, as one woman put it, "that awful ping in the stomach."

Here are some of the best strategies I've learned for fighting your inner critic:

- Know that the more you do something, the less terrifying it will become and the less afraid you'll feel. This is what you discover when it comes to public speaking. The first time you give a speech, you wonder if you should bring a motion sickness bag on the platform with you, but do it enough and there's a chance you will come to love it.

- Don't worry about knowing everything perfectly; instead work at knowing several things very, very well. This is a strategy that Valerie Perlowitz, founder of Women in Technology, said helped her thrive as one of the early women in tech. "As with anything that you do for your work, you need to be sure of yourself, which comes from knowing 'everything' about your industry." While that seems overwhelming, the best way to accomplish it is to know a lot about three to four items in your field and the rest of the topics just well enough to make it appear that you're aware of what's being discussed. This is a great way to network because you can speak to many topics and are an expert in a few, which makes you someone that everyone wants to talk with.

- When you have imposter feelings, remind yourself of what you *do* know (in fact, you may know more than anyone in the room on that subject), *and*, says psychologist Dale Atkins, acknowledge what you *don't* know. "It can be relaxing to differentiate that. You're not expected to know everything. But focus on your own expertise."

- Steal this trick from the Navy SEALs. Apparently they learn to use positive self-talk during challenging and harrowing encounters, and this can work for us mere mortals, too. Come up with a mantra like, "I totally know my stuff and I'm going to rock this presentation today."

- Steal this trick that actress Natalie Dormer (*Game of Thrones*, *Hunger Games*) once shared with me. She learned it from an older actor and began using it for auditions early in her career.

Instead of worrying that you won't be liked or that other people may think negatively of you, focus on everything that you can bring to the situation and how you might be the solution to their problems. For instance, the product or idea you are pitching may positively change the direction of their business.

- Steal this trick from the fabulous Nely Galán, the first Latina president of US television network Telemundo and author of the *New York Times* bestseller *Self Made* (I love this book!). I met Nely when we both spoke at Coca-Cola's terrific women's conference and she told me that she would never have done as well if she'd followed the old adage "Just be yourself." She built her own confidence by channeling the confidence and energy of people she admired and considered brave and empowered. "I call this 'acting as if,'" she told me. "It's not about being fake," she says. "It's more like a shortcut to confidence when you're feeling intimidated."

Sorry Not Sorry

Good girls do a lot of apologizing. They apologize for interrupting a meeting to share a brilliant idea or for going after a promotion because they know a friend at work wants it, too. A recruiter friend of mine in the financial world says that women she interviews often apologize for not being perfect candidates for the position they're applying for. They say things like, "I know my background isn't exactly what you're looking for but a friend in the company encouraged me to apply."

And Terri Wein, cofounder and partner of Weil & Wein, a national career advisory and executive coaching firm, says that women often apologize, too, when they ask for a raise. A woman might say, "I think it may be time for a raise. I know it may seem like a lot of money and I'm sorry to ask for it, but..."

Stop apologizing!

Sure, when called for, apologizing is necessary, but when it's habitual and you blurt it out at every turn, it sends up a red flag of insecurity and lack of confidence and translates as "I'm undeserving." This kind of thinking can undercut the impression you want to give and throw you off course.

Some things not to be apologetic about:

- Throwing out an idea without being called on
- Offering an opinion that's different from someone else's
- Snagging a promotion
- Snagging a promotion a coworker was after, too
- Wanting a great raise
- Getting a better raise than a friend on the staff
- Not being 100 percent perfect for a potential job
- Leveraging several job offers at the same time
- Making a lot of money
- Being fiercely ambitious

Why You Need Executive Presence

In Chapter 4, I talked about the importance of dress and grooming in relation to success. But as you evolve in your career, you also need to develop something called *executive presence*, and it's broader than just your clothes, makeup, and hair.

According to a 2012 study by the Center for Talent Innovation, executive presence accounts for 26 percent of what it takes to secure a promotion. The study points out that it involves not only developing the appropriate appearance but also mastering the art of communication. You need to be a great speaker, know how to command a room, and be able to read an audience. These elements interact to generate an aura of authority. Executive presence *alone* won't score you a promotion, the study indicates, but the lack of it can impede your progress, especially if you're female and/or a person of color.

So:

- **Evaluate your appearance.** Are you truly dressing and gearing your appearance for the job you aspire to? If not, *make adjustments*. Note how the stars in your field look. Emulate them.
- **Take a public speaking class.** And then take a refresher course every year.
- **Take advantage of every chance you have to give a speech or presentation,** even if it scares the hell out of you in the beginning. The more speaking you do, the more skilled you'll become.
- **Don't read a speech.** Write it, commit it roughly to memory, then put keys points on a notecard and talk from those. Conversational is almost always better.
- **When you give any kind of presentation or talk, hold eye contact with people, one at a time, for at least four seconds.** Your natural tendency, especially if you're nervous, will be to let your gaze wander across heads, but this won't give you command of the room; good eye contact will. In the beginning this will feel a little scary, and you'll worry people think you are doing a *Children of the Corn* thing, but in time it will feel totally natural and the audience will respond enthusiastically. A speech coach taught me this tip years ago and it works fabulously.

- **Learn to read a room.** Economist Sylvia Ann Hewlett, who spearheaded the executive presence study (her book *Executive Presence* is a terrific resource), says that we have the means today, thanks to the Internet, to find out a ton about people we're encountering. "Do research in advance if you're meeting with people for the first time. Find the connectors you have with people who will be in that room so you can best cater to their needs." Maybe you're both from the same part of the country or played the same sport in college. *Mention* that. Also, pay attention to body language. If people's attention is flagging, boost your energy level. Or interact more.
- **Practice giving your opinion.** According to the Lean In/ McKinsey study, fewer women in organizations are turned to for their input than men. Make people in your company aware that you have smart opinions and that you are eager to share them.

How to Bring Up an Idea at a Meeting and Not Be Ignored

At a conference I attended not long ago, I had the chance to chat with Kim Reynolds, the lieutenant governor of Iowa, and one of the topics we discussed was how frustrating it is to bring up an idea at a meeting only to have it totally ignored, as if people didn't even hear it. Then five minutes later, you listen in complete frustration as a male colleague raises the SAME idea and it receives an enthusiastic response.

If that happens, you may be the victim of office politics or even gender bias, but in certain cases, the blame may lie with you. You may have failed to present the idea effectively enough for people to really hear you, or you had so much explanation on the front end that no one understood what your point was. Here's how to up your chances of being heard and responded to.

First, never go to a meeting cold. Prepare in advance, even rehearsing points you want to make, and do as much due diligence as possible about the agenda and the participants. "I would always try to game a meeting first," says retired FBI executive Lauren Anderson. "I'd get a sense of the key person's agenda and the agendas of my colleagues in the room and speak to them without seeming obvious. It also serves to show others, subtly or not, that you're interested in their perspectives, needs, wants, and not only your own, which sends a powerful message."

Pick the right spot at the conference table. You don't want to be far away from the person in charge, but you also probably don't want to be right next to him either. "If you sit right *next* to your boss," says Dr. Judith Hall, a distinguished professor of psychology at Northeastern with a specialty in interpersonal and nonverbal communication, "it means he or she will hardly ever look at you."

She recommends instead sitting across from the boss if you're at a small table, or two seats down, kind of in the middle, if you're at a conference table and your boss is at the head (see diagram on page 143). "Until it's time to speak, keep good eye contact with your boss throughout the meeting," she says, even as you're taking notes. "You want to seem fully engaged."

Think props. Anderson says that she's a big believer in making sure your space at the meeting table is opened up and not crowded. "I always brought props—a beverage, pad of paper, phone, etc., and spread out a little. I also did this physically, by keeping my arms fairly open on the table, instead of hands tucked in my lap or under the table. Owning your space transmits confidence and sends the message that you won't be intimidated."

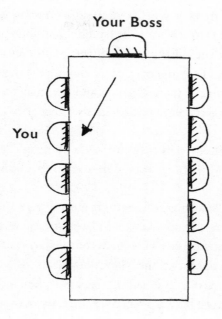

When you're ready to share an opinion or idea, take a second to gain the floor. Rather than just announcing your idea, make a comment like, "I have an idea that could save us five percent in shipping costs," and be sure you have people's attention before continuing.

Then, speaking in a voice loud enough to be heard, cut to the chase immediately with your idea or comment. Try to sum things up in a couple of sentences. "It's good to do your homework, but women sometimes become overly concerned with showing they've done so when they're presenting," says Hewlett. "Don't throw a lot of data at them. Get to the essence or value added. Two sentences often work perfectly."

If you're offering your opinion, go for it with as much gutsiness as you can summon. Sarah Friar says she advises younger women to imagine a scale with 1 being no backbone and 10 being obnoxious, and then to aim for 10. "Because if you aim for 10," she says, "you will end up at 7, whereas if you aim for 7, you will end up at only 5."

Never, Hewlett says, underestimate the importance of body language. "That really feeds into how we present. You need to keep your spine straight, make eye contact, and not get lost in your notes."

Also recognize the power of not overtalking, says Hewlett. "Surrounding important points with silence can be extremely effective."

End strong. Screenwriter Sarah Heyward says she learned this from watching her boss Lena Dunham in action. "She never lets a sentence dangle," says Heyward. "She always finds a way to complete her thought, and she sounds articulate and intelligent as a result. I completely stole that strategy from her and it comes in handy whenever I have a pitch, a meeting, or an interview."

And if someone does manage to hijack your idea, it's best not to blurt out, "Hey, that was *my* idea." It only makes you seem defensive, even desperate. Instead say something like, "I'm glad to hear that referenced again. It's an important idea." That way you still have partial ownership.

How to Stop an Interrupter in His Tracks

Just as men don't often "hear" our ideas in meetings, they also interrupt us, particularly, research shows, in male-dominated settings. And being a gutsy woman is in itself not a safeguard.

According to an empirical study published in *Harvard Business Review*, the male justices on the Supreme Court interrupted the female justices approximately *three times* as often as they interrupted each other during oral arguments.

Here's a trick to stop an interruption short, courtesy of Harris Ginsberg, founder and managing principal of a leadership and executive coaching consultancy. He says he saw a female leader use this flawlessly.

"Lift your hand, palm forward, and say: 'Let me finish my thought, please. I'm almost done and then I'll be glad to give you the floor.' "

The Language of Power and How to Learn It

Part of owning your ambition is recognizing what's required to advance and being ready and willing to learn the skills that you need.

In recent years, companies have stressed the importance of people skills in management training programs, but according to Susan Colantuono, CEO of Leading Women, a consulting firm supporting corporate initiatives to advance women, that kind of emphasis only gets you so far. Her company's research has shown that it's only part of what it takes for women to reach the C-suite.

"We've found that companies overplay the importance of certain skills and activities, like being good with a team, self-promoting, and acquiring a mentor," she says. "Actually, you just need to be good enough at those. That's not what you need to get to the top."

What is, then?

"You need to understand the fundamentals of the business," she says. "You have to know where your company is headed and your role in helping it get there. You have to think like a CEO by developing business, strategic, and financial acumen. That acumen allows you to help achieve the company's financial goals and sustain extraordinary outcomes."

Without this acumen, Colantuono stresses, you are far less likely to be viewed as having leadership potential. She faults companies, in part, for not emphasizing to female employees the acquirement of business acumen. It's sometimes seen as a given that you'll have it. Men, she believes, often develop this acumen through the positions they're encouraged to take and informal mentorship.

The chart on p. 146 offers some of Colantuono's best strategies for developing the acumen you need. Once you learn them, weave your knowledge into what your team does and also tie it to the big outcome when you discuss your team's performance with higher-ups.

The language of power isn't always money-related. Depending on the field, it can involve a certain type of experience, such as IT skills. *Wonder Woman* director Patty Jenkins has said that the ten years she spent doing camera work made it easier for film executives to see she could "handle tech stuff" and direct movies.

Four Ways to Increase Your Clout

Your title and responsibilities alone won't guarantee your stature in the company. You have to actively work to develop and secure your clout.

1. **Drive profitability.** Almost nothing works as well as this.
2. **Feel entitled to information and people that matter.** When I started in my first editor in chief job, I knew little about circulation data. And why would I? I'd never had an opportunity to learn it. As the months went by, the circulation department would share when an issue was up or down on the newsstand and how renewals were doing,

but they rarely offered more. Though these people didn't outrank me, they seemed to live by a code that editors shouldn't be exposed to certain circulation data because it might make them hyper (or even hysterical!). In hindsight I realize I had every right to this information at that point and it would have been so smart for me to set up a series of meetings where the basics were explained, as well as monthly meetings for me to review all the important data. Recognize what you need to know and set things in motion to acquire it. Reach out to the people who can offer you insight.

3. **Keep building alliances.** In her leadership character assessment study, CDR Assessment Group president Nancy Parsons found that successful women executives tended to forge strong alliances that helped them win the perception game and navigate to higher levels. So foster these work friendships and alliances. Second your peers' good ideas. Pass along info that's valuable for them to have in their work. Befriend people on your level in other departments. Have coffee or lunch with them. Shoot them congratulatory emails when they have big wins. Use company events to get to know those on your boss's level in other departments.

4. **Keep being a risk agent and disrupter.** Even a risk that doesn't turn into a home-run can end up enhancing your reputation if it demonstrates how inventive and forward thinking you are.

Two Success Blockers and How to Handle Them

So many good things happen when you finally own your ambition, but it's almost inevitable that you will meet resistance along the way, particularly when someone seems vaguely—or not so vaguely—threatened by your achievements. Here are two tricky problems that can turn up.

Your boss appears to be stymying your success. I was fortunate in the magazine business to have great bosses who seemed invested in my career, but there's no guarantee of that in life. It's not your boss's job to be your mentor or help your career. Unfortunately you can sometimes end up with a boss who actually seems to be *thwarting* you. This kind of boss may praise your work and give you choice assignments but does nothing to promote you to higher-ups and may even take credit for some of your achievements. Or it could simply be a boss who's not effective and you fear you will be tainted by this person's weak performance.

A friend of mine who is a university fund-raiser had a boss who seemed totally supportive of her until a small project she took over began performing beyond anyone's wildest dreams. The president of the university wanted a presentation on the project and my friend's boss suggested that he give the first half of the presentation and she give the second. But when it was her turn, he just *kept going*, making it appear as if she wasn't really involved.

In a situation like this, you may wonder if it would be smart to start doing end runs around your boss, presenting ideas as much as possible to *his* boss. That can be tempting, but it's a potentially dangerous strategy.

What you can do, however, is network with people higher up in the organization, making contacts and even finding sponsors. Approach these people (you should do this even if you have a *good* boss) at company and industry events, even in the elevator.

Comment on one of their successes or ask a smart question. If this person engages you in a Q and A, talk about your department, praising your boss if it's warranted. If your boss is ineffectual, try to take on projects that are beneficial to the department and will develop your knowledge and skills. Boss incompetence can turn into an opportunity for you to grow.

Ideally, your networking and/or special projects will position you for a new role in the company sooner rather than later. If not, look outside. Stingy, threatened, or lame bosses rarely improve, and often the only option is to go elsewhere and find a boss who supports you. There are plenty of them.

Men in your department or company are boxing you out by participating in all-male activities. Even in fields that aren't male dominated, guys are known to do this. They play golf together or go to sporting events and don't invite female coworkers along. Problem is: bonding, networking, information sharing, and idea generating often happen on these occasions. What to do? I recently saw an article where the expert advised going to HR. "Why tiptoe around and run to HR?" says Lauren Anderson. "Put on your big-girl pants, maybe go up to a couple of guys, and say, 'I hope the game was fun; I'd love to go next time.' Or come up with other ideas that might be fun for everyone to do outside the office."

How to Make Girl Power One of Your Secret Weapons

There really is strength in numbers. So work it. Is your company one of many today that offers a women's conference or women's leadership committee? Take part, network, form alliances. You should also join female networking organizations in your field and city. Even create your own small group and share information, concerns, and strategies over dinner.

And foster girl power in your own workplace as well. A top recruiter I know in the financial world believes in what she refers to as the female buddy system. "You look out for each other, have each other's backs," she advises. "It doesn't even have to be a super formal thing. Let's say you're going to be attending a meeting where you plan to pitch an idea but there'll be at least one guy in attendance who loves to hog the floor and act dismissive toward your input. If there's a female you like and trust who'll also be at the meeting, ask her if you can run your idea by her in advance. When I've done this, that woman almost always validates my idea in the meeting and makes a difference."

A Gutsy Girl Manages Her Success, Not Just Her Job

When your career really starts to take off, you can become so busy managing your job responsibilities that you neglect to manage your success. You have to be the relentless architect of your career.

How do you do that? I suggest you build in thirty minutes every single week to take a look your work, your brand, your success. Are you happy with what you're doing? Are you ready for a new challenge? Do you love your work but find yourself in a toxic environment? Are you working so hard that you aren't enjoying life? Research shows that striving can become a bad habit.

If you aren't where you'd like to be professionally, reexamine your brand and your core values. Chunk things down. Define realistic, attainable steps that can bring you closer to the success that you want—on your terms.

Then set a timetable to make that happen. If you need them, here are four key career-boosting moves:

1. **Keep strengthening your strengths.** I mentioned this Marcus Buckingham strategy earlier in the book, and I'm a big believer in it. One of the best things I ever did professionally was take a job midcareer as a senior editor at a kind of shabby Sunday newspaper supplement called *Family Weekly*, where I ended up editing hundreds and hundreds of articles on a wide variety of subjects. It may not have been glamorous, but it really sharpened my editing skills and gave me enormous confidence. And want to hear something amazing? Editors who worked there, myself included, went on to be editors in chief of the following magazines: *Sports Illustrated*; *Philadelphia*; *GQ*; *Redbook*; *McCall's*; *Working Woman*; *Child*; *Cosmopolitan*; *O, the Oprah Magazine*; *American Health*; *Seventeen*; and *Esquire*. I don't think any other magazine ever turbocharged so many careers. Strength strengthening paid off big for all of us.

   And what about your weaknesses? Neutralize them where possible; manage around them by effective delegating.

   That has been the successful strategy of Maria Buttler, who runs Microsoft's sales operations for the consumer and devices business. "When I was CFO of Microsoft Singapore," says Buttler, "I had to sign off on the tax return and I was ultimately accountable for its accuracy, but I relied heavily on tax experts to guide me in preparation. Similarly when I moved to the US and saw issues that might give rise to taxable events, I knew enough to identify them, but would seek expert advice. It's a choice. I could have gone deep and learned tax law in each country I lived in, but I decided to focus on other areas that I was naturally better at. I love leading and developing teams and I love getting deep into the businesses that I'm involved in to help them grow and drive profitability."

2. **Do your career math.** When did successful people in your field hit certain marks? Your blueprint doesn't have to perfectly match up with theirs, but it's good to know about industry "norms" and perceptions. Sometimes, windows close.

3. **Power network.** Never go to an event wondering whom you might meet. Find out in advance who will be there and give yourself a game plan. Who would you kill to meet? Once you're there, make every effort to make contact. Offer your business card and ask for one in return. Attend every networking event with the goal of coming back with a certain number of contacts, as well as at least one fabulous idea.

4. **Go to lunch with an ask. A straightforward one.** Guys know how to do this. They don't get together with mentors, sponsors, or industry pals just to chitchat. They *ask*. For info, for insight, for email or in-person introductions to be made. Do the same.

Why You're Probably a Lot More Ready Than You Believe You Are

One of the worst things that can happen in your career is seeing someone else score an amazing opportunity and thinking, "That would have been so great for *me*." And maybe the reason it didn't happen is because, despite how ambitious you are, you didn't raise your hand for it. I love this quote: "Opportunities missed are options picked up by others." Let me say it again: Opportunities missed are options picked up by others.

If you failed to raise your hand in the past for one or more fabulous opportunities, I bet I can guess the reason. You convinced yourself you weren't ready for it. Or even fully deserving.

You have to stop letting your fear of readiness hold you back. I think the first step is recognizing that when you find yourself hesitating to pursue an opportunity—whether a big assignment at work, a promotion, or a new job—and you're all churned up trying to justify that reluctance, it's often a sign that you really *do* want it badly, but fear of failure is convincing you otherwise.

And once you accept how much you want it, you have to also recognize this very important fact: **You do not have to be 100 percent ready to go after it.**

Have you heard about that study that shows that women tend to go after promotions only when they feel they meet 100 percent of the criteria, whereas guys typically go after one when they meet only 60 percent of the criteria? Though this stat appears in several books and is often cited in articles, it turns out there's been no such study. It was apparently extrapolated from a comment made by a male executive at the consulting firm McKinsey & Company. But, hey, let's face it—the guy was *right*. Woman so often feel they have to be totally and completely prepared, to have all their ducks in a perfect row. No one is actually saying that!

Here's my advice. When it comes to a promotion, new job, or major opportunity, **start before you're ready**. Or *feel* ready. Executive coach Terri Wein says that it's not about whether you have all the skills necessary for the job but whether you can learn them. "When throwing your hat in the ring for a new job, say yes," she advises, "then figure out how to do it. For most positions, applicants have some of the qualifications but not all. If you are smart and a quick study, you can learn the job."

Is there something right now that you've been telling yourself you're not ready to do? Switch your MO.

Instead of: **"Ready, aim, fire."**

Think: **"Aim, fire, ready."**

Just go for it. And it will make a huge difference in your career.

Key Gutsy Girl Takeaways

- Instead of being worried about what people will think of you, focus on what information you are bringing to the meeting or presentation, and what value it has for people.
- Bring up ideas without hesitation, qualification, or apology.
- Think like a CEO. That means gaining business acumen and using it. Know how your area contributes to the bottom line of the company.
- Manage your career and your success as well as your job.
- Start before you're ready. You don't have to be 100 percent prepared for a promotion or a new job. It's *supposed* to be a stretch.

CHAPTER 9

A Gutsy Girl Becomes a Kickass Boss

If you take a totally gutsy approach to your job and your career, it's almost guaranteed that one day you will be in charge. In charge of people, in charge of an important area in your company, in charge, even, of a company itself.

All your gutsy strategies will have helped you arrive here, but now you need those strategies more than ever. Being a boss and a leader is exhilarating, fun, liberating (*you* call the shots), and rewarding, but there are lots of challenges, which in the beginning can seem particularly daunting. You're going to have to deliver big results to *your* boss, inspire and supervise the people who work for you, navigate sometimes intense office politics, and keep your cool throughout.

One of the best ways to learn how to be a gutsy, kickass leader is to reflect on the best bosses you've had. What did they do brilliantly? What, if any, were their shortcomings? Also take full advantage of any training programs or executive coaching your company offers.

In the meantime, here are strategies that you can use to your advantage.

Kickass Bosses Always Start with a Mission and a Plan

When you're a boss and a leader, you absolutely must have a vision for what you hope to accomplish and a plan to make it happen.

If you're running a department or division of a company, your mission will reflect the overall company mission. In some cases a mission will be handed to you, and you'll want to gain as much clarity as possible on it from your boss. Set up meetings, listen, and articulate what your takeaway is.

In other situations you may be given free rein to create your own mission for a department or area, as long as it fits with the overall goals of the company and drives profitability. When I first became head of an articles department at a magazine, my boss told me to just "make the articles exciting." Whether you're developing your own mission or executing one handed to you, do your homework. Gather data and talk to your new direct reports. (My best advice: In the beginning, eschew group meetings with direct reports, which can be deadly and unproductive, and speak with your top staffers one-on-one.)

In his fabulous book *The First 90 Days: Proven Strategies for Getting Up to Speed Faster and Smarter* (a must-read for any new boss/leader), author Michael D. Watkins points out the danger in succumbing to the urge to quickly just *do something*. You must take time to learn and get up to speed, not assuming when you start that you have the answer. Watkins says to aim for "actionable insights...knowledge that enables you to make better decisions earlier." This insight will help you shape your mission and determine what your priorities should be in terms of first steps.

I've always believed it can help to boil your mission down to a statement, just as you did your professional brand. *Cosmo*'s vision/

mission was summed up in the tagline *Fun Fearless Female*, and it was a fabulous tool to work with. I held those three words up to everything that crossed my desk—ideas, fashions, photos, events, etc.—and if they didn't fit perfectly, I passed. And I regularly reminded my staff of those words. In keeping those three words in mind, we didn't try to be all things to all young women. Examples of content you wouldn't find in *Cosmo* included earnest articles, cutesy lists, and sensible fashion. Occasionally a certain frustration arose from having such a clearly defined but tight vision, like when our nearest competitor ran interviews with the presidential candidates and we chose not to because I knew *Cosmo* readers weren't turning to us for that type of feature (even though they might like to read it elsewhere). By adhering to our mission, though, we ended up outselling our nearest competitor by over a million copies each month on the newsstand.

Sometimes people will try to lure or push you off your mark, but stick to your guns. "Stay true to yourself and what you believe," says former CEO Bobbi Brown. "In my early days of business, I was persuaded to change course and launch a collection of super neon colors. It was a disruption to my nudes, which is what I was known for. Needless to say, it didn't work."

Once you feel confident in your mission, determine the first actions you need to take to make that mission a reality. Again, this will come from homework. Aim to secure what Watkins calls *early wins*. "By the end of the first few months," he writes, "you want your boss, your peers, and your subordinates to feel that something new, something good, is happening." Resist the urge to address problems that are easy to fix but detract from more important business.

"When I joined Jamba Juice, they'd just relocated their headquarters from California to Texas, with only about ten percent of employees transferring with the move," says Jamba Juice's

Marie Perry. "It was imperative to attract and hire the right talent for these positions. One of my earliest wins was the ability to identify and complete an A team in accounting, legal, and human resources. Having the right talent has paid off tenfold."

Your mission may change, of course, as you continue to learn critical info, or the market changes. Be flexible.

Sixteen Other Gutsy Boss Moves

1. **Lead and learn.** Never stop acquiring info. Pick the brains of experts in the field. Take workshops. If you've got the budget, hire short-term consultants. Early in my days as an editor in chief, I paid direct-response copywriters to teach me their brilliant tricks so I could become better at writing compelling cover lines. Once I even hired a numerologist to illuminate for me how people responded to numbers (should it be "100 Best Sex Tips Ever" or "99"?). Don't waste your money on that one!

   And if you're new in the company, be sure you invest a big chunk of time in learning about the culture. How are things done there? What's a no-no? I've seen several very smart, capable people fail in big jobs because they didn't pay any heed to how the new culture was different from where they'd worked previously.

2. **Be a baller as a leader, too.** Arrive at work ahead of your team. Don't sit on things. Make decisions instantly as often as possible. Give clear instructions—with deadlines.

3. **Make your boss a top priority.** When you've been given the chance to be in charge of an area, it can be easy at moments to lose track of your boss. Don't! Figure out her priorities and make sure you're communicating in a

style she favors (e.g., face-to-face, phone, or email). As Michael Watkins points out, it's key that your early wins matter not just to you but also to your boss.

4. **Dare to hire people unlike yourself.** You never want to have subordinates who buck your vision, but you do want people reporting to you who bring skills you don't have, different sets of experience, and fresh perspective. Provide clear direction and expectations, giving them as much autonomy as possible. Don't breathe down their necks.

5. **Be fair but don't feel you have to be one of them or play down your own power.** A sociologist once told me that people *want* to be directed. It relaxes them to know that someone is leading them, and without that they feel nervous.

6. **Aim to bring out the best in the people who work for you and reward strong performance.** Give them assignments they will relish. Share your insider thinking and strategies. Praise them. In writing sometimes. A shout-out to *your* boss about the person. Sometimes go beyond that. A gift certificate. A chance to attend a special event in the company. When someone really excels, offer a terrific new assignment or promotion. Tell them, "You'd be great at this. Go do it."

7. **But also foster healthy competition.** Though employees want you to treat them respectfully, they also thrive when there's healthy competition. Send out a memo praising a particular employee's accomplishment. Give the person with the great idea a chance to present it elsewhere in the company.

8. **Ask for feedback and discourage "yes" people, but don't always aim for consensus.** Deborah Tannen, the highly regarded professor of linguistics at Georgetown, once told me that men are driven by a need to achieve and

maintain the upper hand, while women seek to confirm and support—and to reach consensus. Don't succumb to a need for consensus. If you disagree with a staffer's suggestion, simply say you appreciate the input, but your instincts are taking you in a different direction.

9. **Discuss performance or behavior issues with subordinates immediately.** Don't wait. The problem won't go away. Give the person a chance to speak and try to figure out their motivation and whether you may not have articulated your needs clearly enough.

10. **Don't be in denial about the people who aren't really on board.** I recently heard a female executive make this very valid point: "People who work for you are either rowing the boat or drilling holes in the back." You can't ignore the hole drillers.

In certain instances, a subordinate will put up resistance to your agenda simply because he doesn't like the idea of you being the boss. Perhaps he's much older than you, or just a year younger, or it's a guy who has a hard time with the idea of a woman boss. Ignore at your own peril. Acknowledge to the person that you see the resistance and it's not acceptable. It's occasionally possible to bring this type of person along by letting him see that your leadership will ultimately pay off for him personally—for instance, by giving the person "stretch" assignments, opportunities to grow.

In other instances, people get caught up in the way things used to be done and you have to tell them, "I know there was a certain comfort in the way things used to be done, but we're shifting and everyone has to shift, too." Meet with resisters. They may be open to changing or you both have to acknowledge that it's not a good fit anymore.

11. **Hold crisp meetings.** Keep them small, only inviting those whose attendance is absolutely necessary. (Personally, I've never been in an effective meeting that had more than five people.) Also, keep them as short as possible. Have an agenda of the points you want addressed. Don't allow interruptions or distractions. Expect timeliness, and start without people who are late. Expect participation and realize that people who take the discussion off course often do so because they aren't prepared. Call them on it privately later.

12. **Keep building alliances within the company.** Do this particularly with company leaders and peers in other departments. You will need them now more than ever. Share your vision. Share guidance and information. Support their ideas. And don't restrict alliances to people at your level or above. People on all sorts of levels, including support staff, can be resources for information and insight if you take the time to get to know them (hey, over the years I acquired a few valuable pieces of information from building security guards!).

13. **Pay close attention to any shift in *your* boss's mission/ vision, and make sure your mission/vision aligns with that.**

14. **Dare to be self-aware.** Research shows that high achievers often take too much credit for their success and assign too much *external* blame for their failures.

15. **Fire people who you realize will never deliver.** Otherwise they will drag you down.

16. **Let your passion show.** "When you love your job, it's contagious," says Dr. Ellen Marmur.

Wait, One More! Number 17: The Surprising Secret of the Best and Gutsiest Bosses

If someone asked me to picture a gutsy woman in action, I'd probably imagine her at the front of a room, commanding everyone's attention. Maybe she'd be leading a meeting or giving a presentation, dazzling every listener with her remarks.

But here's a point that at first sounds almost counterintuitive. One of the gutsiest things you can do as a boss and leader is just shut the hell up and listen.

"When we're the boss, we tend to believe our job is to tell people what to do and to look like we have all the answers," says Hal Gregersen, executive director of the MIT Leadership Center and a senior lecturer in leadership and innovation at the MIT Sloan School of Management. "We think, 'I've got to be right, and that means talkative, verbal.'"

The problem with that approach is that it can put you in a good-news bubble, where people neglect to share bad but critical-to-know info. Smart leaders, Gregersen told me, develop deeply inquisitive leadership practices and stay on the lookout for both passive data and active data.

It's a matter, he says, of finding out what you don't know as well as *what you don't know you don't know*. Some strategies that will help:

- **Practice being quiet.** There's a good chance that this may not come naturally (sometimes as an editor in chief I had to force myself to clamp my lips shut!). Sit still as the person speaks, maintain eye contact, and nod to show you are paying attention.

- **Don't rush to fill in the blanks.** Wait a beat after some-one answers in case she has more to say but is feeling ner-vous and hesitant.
- **Get into the habit, Gregersen says, of asking "What's working?" "What's not working?" and "Why?" or "Why not?"**
- **Take notes.** That's what Pfizer exec Sally Susman does. "I listen best by taking notes," she says, "picking up on big ideas and key words. I always keep the notes, and have made a habit of reviewing them for patterns and mean-ing. This can be especially useful in a larger organization, where leaders often serve in cross-functional roles. Listen-ing to a common theme emerge across divisions can give you valuable insight into the most pressing priorities."
- **When the news isn't good, avoid responding in a nega-tive, knee-jerk way.** Remain neutral, ask questions. Let the person see that it's safe to share.

Listening isn't just about hearing people talk. It's about walk-ing the floor and observing. It's about looking at information and data that people provide (especially when you're new) and being truly curious, even if it runs contrary to some of your thinking.

Drain the Swamp as You Slay the Alligators

This expression is actually derived from an old Southern saying that goes something like this: "When you're up to your ass in gnats and alligators, it can be hard to remember that your origi-nal goal was to drain the swamp." In other words: You shouldn't get so caught up in the day-to-day that you fail to address the big-picture goals. Ignore those and you will never triumph.

I owe so much of my success at *Cosmo* to ruthlessly making myself do this every week. I scheduled the time without fail on my calendar and I used it to learn as much as I could about readers, consider their needs, and decide how to make the magazine relevant to them, constantly introducing new features and columns.

You need to set up at least an hour every week—and I mean *religiously*—to "drain the swamp," think about your overall vision/mission, generate go-big ideas that will ensure its evolution and success, and make sure you're not drifting from it. Block out this time on your calendar and let nothing interfere.

Become a Legend in Your Time

Success comes not simply from doing a dazzling job but from becoming known for doing a dazzling job. You need to create the *story* of you—an exciting, compelling story that people latch on to. And you need to begin doing this in the early days of your new role as boss. "It used to be that you needed a third party to create your story, like a PR firm," says PR guru Deb Shriver. "But now you can be the creator and distributor. For instance, do you want to be known as 'the rescuer'? Or 'the turnaround artist'? Be consistent, push it out on social media if appropriate, and know that it's not just about what you include but what you leave out."

Michael Watkins says to use teachable moments to reinforce your story. "These are actions that clearly display what you are about," he writes. "They can be as simple, and as hard, as asking the penetrating questions that crystalize your group's understanding of a key problem the members are confronting." Shriver says she knows a twenty-nine-year-old in sports marketing who has become known as "NOB," meaning Not on Brand, for always using that simple phrase, "not on brand," to nix concepts that don't fit with the company's mission.

Using sound bites can be another way to reinforce the story of you, what you're all about. UN ambassador Nikki Haley is a particular master of this. Two examples within her first months on the job: "I wear heels, and it's not for a fashion statement. It's because if I see something wrong, we're gonna kick 'em every time." And, "For those that don't have our backs, we're taking names."

If you're a leader, "you need to learn how to create pithy sound bites," says Margaret Milkint, who heads the Jacobson Group's executive search property.

When I think back on my best bosses, they all did this. It not only grabbed attention but also reinforced the person's story/brand. For instance, when Cathie Black took over as president of the magazine division of Hearst while I was running *Redbook*, she told us at a management conference that she intended to "blow the dust off the curtains of the magazine division." No specifics, just that one striking sound bite. It suggested there would be fresh ideas as well as a fresh way of doing business, yet, thankfully for all of us, it didn't sound as if she intended to burn the house down. You wanted to jump on board.

Milkint's tips for a great sound bite:

- Avoid disclaimers like "I'm not the expert here, but..."
- Make it focused and direct.
- Use actionable words.
- Make it visual.

The Cathie Black line I mentioned above is a perfect example. Focused, visual, with a clear action in mind.

Focused, direct, one sentence long

"We're going to (blow) the
↑action word
(dust off the curtains) here."
→ visual

Provocative without being threatening

How to Be the Best Kind of HBIC

In Chapter 1, I discussed the importance of knowing the four B's. But there's another *B* word that needs to be discussed, and that's BITCH. You can be called a bitch at many points in your career, but it's when you're in a leadership role that being pegged that way can have the biggest consequences.

The awesome Gloria Steinem once said that if someone calls you a bitch, you should say, "Thank you." She makes a great point with that comment. Women often get labeled as bitchy not because they really are bitches in the nasty sense of the word (people who make their subordinates' work lives a living hell) but simply for being blunt, decisive, tough-minded, and unafraid to kick butt and take names when necessary. Isn't that something we should be applauded for and feel unapologetic about? After all, isn't that the way a leader needs to be? The Head Bitch in Charge!

It would be nice if we really could just say thank you. But unfortunately, being considered a bitch at work (I'm talking about more than the passing comment from a disgruntled subordinate) can backfire. People don't like working for women they consider bitches. They don't give their best, they withhold critical information, they bad-mouth them around the organization, and they quit for other jobs at the worst possible moments.

But, on the other hand, you can't afford to seem like a pushover.

"Being forceful and assertive are core executive traits to embody," says economist Sylvia Ann Hewlett, author of *Executive Presence*. "But assertiveness can make you unlikeable and then the *B* word gets rolled out. Yet if you're seen as too meek, that's not leadership material either."

Men don't face nearly the same challenge.

"The normal bandwidth of acceptable behavior is just much wider for men than women," says Pattie Sellers, who not only runs her own company but also oversees Fortune's Most Powerful Women conference.

Research by Nancy Parsons has shown that what's labeled as mere overconfidence in men is viewed as being a "self-absorbed bitch" in women, and what's seen in a man as being capable of selling one's point of view is considered being too opinionated in a woman. At the other extreme, being tagged as thoughtful and reserved in a male is viewed as nonassertive in a woman.

So what do you do? One option is to be willing to experiment and then modify. "It may not be fair, but you might have to adapt your style to be acceptable," says Sellers.

But little adjustments shouldn't mean squashing your personality. "I think women gain power by being themselves and stepping into who they are," says executive coach Liz Bentley. "I have a client who is what we call a Big D, meaning very dominant and aggressive, and it works for her. At the same time," Bentley says, "you have to be aware of your audience and be willing, if necessary, to shift slightly to that audience." Two of Bentley's most important guidelines for clients address each end of the spectrum. "Be a gracious leader, someone who approaches situations with grace and dignity," she says. "At the same time, never show your vulnerability. A little self-deprecation is fine, but you can't arrive at work saying something like, 'I had such a huge fight with my husband last night.'"

Sometimes your style will need to depend on the circumstances. "If you're in front of a bunch of crotchety old guys," says Bentley, "you may want to tone things down, but if you're with a group of millennials, you won't have to." Jan Fields, president of McDonald's USA, told me that how you play it depends to some degree on who you want to influence and what you need to accomplish. "Sometimes you want to kick ass," she says. "And sometimes you want to kiss it."

If you sense you're not coming across as effectively as you should, ask your mentor for honest feedback. Reread your evaluation undefensively. Consider working with an executive coach—there are many good ones these days and your company may even pay for it if you ask—who can work with you to find a sweet spot for yourself, one that lets you be you but doesn't push the wrong buttons.

And what if you actually do have a reputation as a bitch and it's undermining you? Consider these tactics for altering perceptions:

- **Humor.** Being funny at the right moments can be a great balance for the times when you have to, in Hewlett's words, show teeth. It demonstrates you're human and approachable as well as tough-minded. Of course, your sense of humor has to be appropriate, shouldn't undercut your authority, and can't be at anyone's expense.

- **Empathy.** Show concern for your subordinates—when they're ill, when one of their family members has been ill, when they're facing a troubling personal issue, when a work project has gone off the rails through no fault of their own. Know that one of their biggest concerns is dealing with the intersection of work and personal life, and if you can help them with that, you will gain many points.

- **The handwritten note.** I've had a bunch of female bosses over the years, most of them really terrific. Among these terrific ones were several who were at times pretty tough but never in a way I considered negative. As I was thinking lately about how they pulled off this balance, I realized that this group had one interesting trait in common: When you did something fabulous, they wrote you a handwritten note singing your praises. Whenever I received one of these, it always knocked my socks off and helped inspire loyalty. Write notes of praise to your wonderful performers. Handwritten ones, not just emails. People will love them. They will even save them.

Ultimately you have to decide how much compromising you want to do and balance it with your career goals. Parsons points out that women who run their own companies have more leeway because they don't have to play by an organization's rules. It's going to come down to what you want for the future.

How to Act When You're Pissed

I have a wonderful friend in the media business who uses a phrase that I love: "Cool always beats hot." Meaning that no matter how furious you are with someone in a work situation, it's best to keep a cool head rather than yell, curse, berate, vent your anger in an email, or tear the person a new you know what. I totally believe this. I almost always regretted the times I gave in to anger, raised my voice, and let someone really have it.

That doesn't mean you should stifle your annoyance with a subordinate when they've been deliberately careless or lazy. But a calm, cool, in some cases even frosty, approach can be far more effective. When you blow up and scream, it's easy for the person to become defensive and fail to accept that your irritation is legitimate. I always learned best from bosses who weren't screamers and expressed their disappointment neutrally.

And here's my two cents on those emails you plan to send when a colleague has really worked your last nerve:

1. When you're drafting the message, don't type in the recipient's address. It's too easy to accidentally hit Send before you've finished composing your thoughts.

2. Sleep on it. At the very least, let several hours pass, giving yourself a chance to cool down and come back to the material with a fresh eye. Is this really, *really* what you want the person to read? Will you feel the same way in three days? What are the possible repercussions? Could it backfire on you?

3. Don't actually send it. If you have something serious to say to a subordinate or colleague, it's far better to do it in person. It's easy for emails to be misinterpreted and/or shared with others.

   Instead, simply use the draft you created as a way of gathering your thoughts and/or letting off steam. Then arrange to talk to the person face-to-face. The end results are likely to be far better.

Two Bad Boss Moves to Use Once in a While

1. **Don't always explain yourself.** I wanted my direct reports to learn from me, so I often shared my reasoning on a decision—for instance, why I'd gone with one top cover line over another.

   But you're not always required to explain or justify a decision. Holding back, particularly if you're a new leader, demonstrates that despite how fair you are, you're still in charge and not everything is open to discussion. Plus, not always offering an explanation can keep employees curious in a good way.

2. **Sometimes completely change your mind.** Good leaders tend to act decisively and stick with their choices. But some of my best bosses sometimes *did* change their minds, upending an action that was already in the works. This kind of behavior, though frustrating at the moment, helped me understand, before I got there myself, that leaders are privy to information from a variety of sources that subordinates aren't always aware of, and that data can compel them to switch course.

Now Inspire Fierce Devotion

A few pages ago, I ran through the seventeen strategies gutsy bosses use. Follow those and people will work hard and relish the experience. But I think that ultimately you want something more from your employees, particularly your top-level people. You want their fierce devotion. You want them to love their jobs so much that they thrive in the environment and turn in not just good results, but great ones. When I was at *Cosmo*, I had a senior team of people who stayed with me for years and knocked my socks off every day. And that played a monster-sized role in why we thrived as the number one women's magazine in the world.

So how do you inspire fierce devotion? Recently I asked my former brand director John Searles (who inspired fierce devotion on *his* part with his direct reports) what he thought the secret was, and I loved his response: "In the *Life-Changing Magic of Tidying Up*, the author Marie Kondo says that the best way to decide whether you keep something or throw it away is to ask, 'Does this item spark joy in me?'" he said. "Maybe a great question to ask yourself as a boss is 'Does my leadership ignite joy and passion in my employees as well as me?'"

I think that nails it. The people who work for you are looking for passion. They want to feel passionate about the work environment, the mission you've laid out, the work they do to accomplish that mission, and the rewards that work brings them. So ask yourself:

- **Have I created a culture people love being part of?** "You can't deny the happiness factor," says Bobbi Brown. "If your employees are happy, they will produce better work. I created a culture in the workplace that made people want to come to work and do a good job. I built a healthy kitchen, and held yoga classes and wellness seminars, and hired an on-site manicurist."
- **Is my own passion contagious?** Have you made the mission exciting and have you shared it clearly? And do you talk about it with full-blown enthusiasm?
- **Have you given people work they can love?**
- **Is there a clear and exhilarating payoff for them?**

How to Get Known Outside the Company

When you're a boss, you have to be all-in with your job. But save time and energy to make your mark in your field and not just the company you work for or the company you own.

How do you do it? "Volunteer," says Deb Shriver. "Donate your time, money, talents. Join a nonprofit board. Host an industry meeting at your workplace and not only help plan the agenda but offer to speak. Share and show off talents to peers in other companies and fields. Word will get around."

If there's no organization for you to join and become involved with, START ONE. In 1994 Valerie Perlowitz, now founding partner of International Holding Company, was talking to a lawyer friend about how difficult it was for her to meet more executive women who worked in technology and simply keep up with all the rapid changes in that field. There was no one organization geared toward making these connections for women. So she decided to start Women in Technology. "My friend had her company lend us space for our kickoff meeting," she says. "When it came time to 'open the doors,' we were surprised that there were almost two hundred women who came to learn about the organization. It was obvious that there had been a vacuum for an organization such as WIT. Its purpose was and still is to provide a place for women to network with their peers and to learn about technology changes. Today, it boasts over two thousand members and has branched out to reach girls to interest them in STEM, provide board training for WIT members, and other functions pertinent to the members."

This is also the point when you should be a mentor to other women. Provide advice and guidance. Make email introductions, and agree to exploratory interviews when time allows. It's giving back, but also enhances your reputation.

As you move up in your career, becoming a member of a board is a terrific way to increase your visibility and stature, and gain expertise. At this time, women constitute only 20 percent of all board members in Fortune 500 companies, so it's not easy. Being a board member of a nonprofit first can increase the likelihood of securing membership on a board for a profit-based company.

Lastly, establish your presence in the outside world. Use the same group of restaurants for business meals and the same hotels when you travel. And tip fabulously. It pays off!

Why Power Can Be Sweeter Than It Looks

A couple years ago, a team of women at Harvard surveyed a diverse sample of more than four thousand people and found that "while women and men believe they are equally able to attain high-level leadership positions, men want that power more than women do." Women, they found, perceive professional power as less desirable than men do.

The researchers—Francesca Gino, a professor in the Negotiations, Organizations and Markets unit of Harvard Business School; Alison Wood Brooks, an assistant professor in the same unit; and Caroline Wilmuth, who was pursuing a doctorate in organizational behavior at Harvard—offered a possible explanation: "Women are more likely than men to feel anxious about the sacrifices or difficult trade-offs they would have to make to give that goal more attention than others. Thus, women may associate power-related goals (such as taking on a high-level position) with more negative outcomes than men (such as not allowing them to attain other important goals in life)—which could help explain why women view a high-level position as less desirable than men do, even if it seems equally attainable."

In another study, the researchers found that compared to male participants, female participants expected a promotion to bring more negative outcomes, which led them to view the potential promotion as less desirable than men did and to be less likely than men to pursue it.

You know what? I really relate to the women in the survey who felt hesitant about power. There have been times during my career when I was on the brink of assuming a top job and ended up feeling my stomach clench in dread. And it wasn't simply that typical female fear of readiness. I was afraid that the new job would get in the way of other goals I'd set for myself, such as being a good mom and wife, traveling, and purely *enjoying* life.

Have you worried about that, too?

Well, here's something I want to share with you, something I learned from running five magazines. Power that looks daunting from the outside can actually be very sweet if you're on the inside. Yes, it comes with its headaches and trade-offs and sacrifices, but it's also fabulously rewarding and can offer you a wonderful sense of freedom and control over your destiny.

You get to call the shots and do things *your* way. When I took over *Cosmo*, I heard the staff worked till 8:00 many nights and that the editor in chief rarely left before then either. I had young kids and didn't want that kind of lifestyle. Well, during my first month, my managing editor and I took a look at the situation and discovered the late hours were simply a result of bad time management and we could adjust that. From then on, I left every day at a totally reasonable hour.

Okay, admittedly I was lucky. I worked for a terrific company with terrific bosses who let me do my thing. But those good companies are out there. Find one. Or start your own.

There's also a ton to be said for the financial benefits (and perks) that power often offers you. You just have more resources at your disposal, which can be of real value on the home front.

So just *try* it. Instead of flinching, go for the top job and discover the pure, glorious thrill and endless rewards of being in charge.

And if it doesn't suit you or you feel it undermines your other goals, you can always walk away.

Key Gutsy Girl Takeaways

- When you're a boss/leader, always start with a clear, dynamic vision.
- Reward your stellar performers.
- Listen more than you talk.
- Drain the swamp as you slay the alligators, building in time to generate big ideas.
- Be willing to adjust your style.
- Inspire fierce devotion.

The Gutsy Girl's Guide to Life

I've spent every page of this book up until now describing how to use a gutsier approach to accomplish the goals you have for your job and your career.

But I don't want to wrap up without addressing the elephant in the room, the subject all working women grapple with: how to keep your professional life from playing havoc with your personal one.

I think by now we all know that work–life balance is a myth. There's no way to perfectly balance those two areas. Work and life overlap a lot and that's not always a bad thing (my kids still say how much they loved helping me select photos for magazine covers and keeping me abreast of celeb trends), but you want to be sure that work issues and deadlines don't constantly muscle their way into your personal life, hijacking your free time and preventing you from fulfilling key personal goals.

When women talk to me about some of the difficulties they experience while trying to keep their personal lives fairly sacred, particularly when they have young kids, I can really relate. Since I first started working, I've attempted to make my personal life my top priority, but it hasn't been easy at certain junctures. My son was just six months old when I took my first editor in chief

job, and I was seven months pregnant with my second child, my daughter, when I accepted my second editor in chief post. There were some really crazy moments along the way, in part because for many years my husband worked nights.

I've always attempted to handle my personal goals and schedule with the same level of gutsiness as I approached my career, but in hindsight I probably could have been even gutsier, borrowing more strategies from my career to truly be the boss of my personal time.

So don't be shy. Don't hold back as I did at times. Be the relentless architect of your personal life, too. You can use all the gutsy girl strategies I laid out in the book in this arena, too. Here are a few examples.

Define your *personal* brand, just as you have your professional brand. What matters most to you? Come up with your core words (such as family, volunteering, cross-training, meditating, learning Italian) and even devise a personal brand statement. With that brand statement in hand, look back over your calendar from the past months. How did you do when it came to scheduling what matters? If not well, work at fixing it. Factor your personal brand statement into how you plan your time and set up your day.

Go big or go home, even if it means breaking the rules. When I was single in my early thirties and running the articles department for a magazine, I began to feel a longing to travel around the world, perhaps for at least a year, but at the same time I worried taking off for that long would derail my career (and I'd be broke at the end). My mom challenged me to come up with a cool alternative, and after brainstorming, I realized that taking longer vacations and going to truly exotic places might satisfy my desire. Problem: No one at the magazine I worked for, including my boss, ever took vacations that lasted more than about ten days. But I decided to investigate the possibility of breaking the ten-day-vacation rule. I went to my boss and asked if she would be willing to let me take three weeks off at a stretch if I enlisted my number two to cover for me. I tried to impress on her that since a big part of my job was producing ideas for the magazine—and I wanted to keep drumming up the best ideas possible—travel would be a fantastic way for me to expand my universe. I'm sure she didn't love my plan, but I was a valued employee and she said yes. Over the next few years, I took some amazing trips, which included several weeks tagging penguins in Patagonia with the World Wildlife Foundation and three weeks helping a professor restore an archeological site in Rarotonga, an enchanting island in the South Pacific.

Be a baller. Once you decide what you want on the personal front, go after it with your A game. That's what Stephanie Libous did when she realized that though she loved her job at a PR firm in New York City, she was dying to live in the UK. The hitch: The firm had a tiny UK office with no openings available, and it would be nearly impossible to get a job through a British company. So she pulled out all the stops to convince her firm to let her work in the London office. With the help of her direct manager and mentor, she spent four months putting a shell of a proposal together. "I included research from *PR Week* and other industry reports for the competitive analysis and market research," she says. "The financial plan was a bit more difficult, but I was able to do an estimated cost analysis of new hires, onboarding, revenue, etc. While it wasn't the most accurate, my boss was impressed that I at least put the effort in to try." The final report was nine pages. The whole process took over a year, but it paid off. She was awarded a job in the UK office as an account manager.

Look for openings, then take them, and if you can't find one, create it. If the obvious route isn't going to work for you for one reason or another, don't just bail altogether. Find a different route or an opening that will at least keep you in the game or that could land you what you want in a different way. Here's a perfect example I heard when movie director Patty Jenkins spoke at a conference recently. Though Jenkins had won raves for directing the Oscar-nominated film *Monster*, after her son was born she decided to take a break from directing movies because they were so demanding of her time. But rather than simply sit out a few years, she found a perfect option: directing TV pilots, which weren't as time-consuming. Her totally compelling pilots for series like *The Killing* and *Betrayal* kept her career hot, helping her to eventually (when she was ready) land the job of directing *Wonder Woman*, which became a staggering success.

In certain cases a potential opening may be disguised as something else. A friend of mine who teaches English in a private school recently convinced her school to fund a plan for her to study for a week at Shakespeare's Globe theater in London. Great learning experience, but also a free trip abroad.

Often an opening is there for you. You just have to look for it and go after it.

Say yes to what matters and no to everything else. Be ruthless. Set boundaries. No one else will set them for you. If taking up piano again is one of your goals, be sure it's there on your calendar every week. Sheri Riley, a former marketing exec who once crafted strategies for stars like Usher and Toni Braxton and now coaches celebrities and corporate executives on how to make choices that lead to less stress, told me that she's a big believer in "creating margins" in her schedule. "Instead of making every minute accounted for," she says, "I leave free time on my schedule, particularly on Fridays. That way I know I have time to just sit and think or say yes to something that matters."

Ask for what you want even if you can think of a good reason not to. Just as it's hard to ask for what we want at work, it's hard to ask in our personal lives, too. We don't want to be seen as needy or greedy, and we can come up with fabulous excuses for not making our needs known. We think, "No one else is doing it, so it must not be possible"; "It's going to be easier to do it myself"; or "They'll get mad if I ask."

Don't talk yourself out of asking. Some great things to ask for:

- More time off from your job (often can be given under the table).
- A longer maternity leave (whenever I could as a boss, I gave longer maternity leaves to new mothers than I was supposed to *under the table*, and I can't be the only person willing to do it).
- Tuition reimbursement for that course that may change your life.
- Help from your partner. (Great advice I learned at *Cosmo*: When asking a man for assistance, be specific, as in "Can you be in charge of the kids' dentist appointments?" and when possible, ask in a note or email.)
- Guidance and help from people.

But when you ask, remember to focus on how your ask will play into the other person's needs, not just your own. Just as in work, if you present a request, the other person is going to wonder what's in it for him. When Stephanie Libous made the case to work in the London office of her PR firm, a key part of her proposal was emphasizing the benefit to the corporate practice, their objectives, and the London office culture.

Stop making it perfect. Please learn from my mistakes on this front. During the crazy years when my kids were young, I invested way too much energy in things like setting cute tables, making complicated meals for company, sending my kids adorable care packages when they were at camp, and being a good hostess when other families came by. I do know my kids fondly recall all the Fourth of July flag cakes I constructed with whipped cream, raspberries, and blueberries, but I am almost certain they would remember a store-bought one just as fondly!

Own your ambition and embrace your readiness. Is your fantasy to move to Key West one day? Yes, you need to consider viability, but don't worry about being 100 percent ready. Aim, Fire, Ready!!

Be a risk agent. I'm all in favor of having a nice comfort zone you can inhabit in your personal life. For me, that's been about hanging with my husband on weekends, seeing my kids whenever I can, eating meals in the backyard, and watching British crime dramas on Netflix. Nothing is going to budge me away from those activities. But working at *Cosmo*, a place that required regular risk-taking, taught me that though risk is scary, the end results are often pretty exhilarating.

Make smart risk-taking a regular part of your life. Nine years ago, my husband and I bought a little house on the beach in Uruguay, where we now spend our winters. We made sure it was a smart risk, but still it was pretty adventurous (more than one person has asked if we have to fly through the Congo to get there). And yet going each year is exhilarating, proof to me of all the benefits risk can bring.

Take risks. In fact, consider taking one every day.

Remember, the rumble starts today. Right here, right now. Not only in your work but also where your work intersects with your personal life. Time to be gutsy as hell.

Acknowledgments

Thank you from the bottom of my heart to all the gutsy girls who, throughout my life, inspired me, had my back, and offered terrific, sometimes badass advice—gutsy girl teachers, college administrators, bosses, coworkers, editors, work connections, friends, daughter Hayley, sisters-in-law, aunts, nieces, cousins, grandmothers, and especially my late, awesome mom.

Thank you to Karen Rosenbaum and Kathy Schneider for encouraging me to revise the original book, to Betty Garret of Garret Speakers International for seconding that idea, and to Anne Bruce for sharing her wisdom.

Thank you to Jamie Raab for jumping on the idea without me even having to ask because you thought of it, too, at almost the exact same moment, and for bringing me back to Grand Central.

Thank you to my amazing agent, Sandy Dijkstra, for encouraging me from the very beginning to run with the idea and for shepherding it through.

And thank you to my terrific editor, Brittany McInerney, for your great guidance and support and for being a dream to work with.

About the Author

Credit: Keith Major

Kate White is the *New York Times* bestselling author of twelve murder mysteries and psychological thrillers, including *Even If It Kills Her,* and several popular career books, including *Why Good Girls Don't Get Ahead…but Gutsy Girls Do.* For fourteen years, White was the editor in chief of *Cosmopolitan* magazine, and she now speaks frequently at companies and conferences. Find out more at katewhite.com and katewhitespeaks.com.